THE
TeddyBear Lovers Catalog

by
Ted Menten

♥

COURAGE BOOKS

Philadelphia, Pennsylvania

Copyright © 1983, 1985 by Ted Menten
Printed in Hong Kong.
All rights reserved under the Pan-American
and International Copyright Conventions.

Canadian representatives: General Publishing Co. Ltd.,
30 Lesmill Road, Don Mills, Ontario M3B 2T6.

9 8 7 6 5 4 3 2

Digit on the right indicates the number of this printing.

Library of Congress Cataloging in Publication Data:
　　Menten, Theodore.
　　　The teddy bear lovers catalog.
　　　Reprint. Originally published: New York: Delilah Books, © 1983.
　　　Includes index.
　　　1. Teddy bears—Juvenile literature.　2. Teddy bears—Catalogs—
　　Juvenile literature.　I. Title.
[GV1220.7.M46　1985]　　　688.7′24　　　85–13311

ISBN: 0-89471-413-9 Cloth

Cover design by Toby Schmidt

This book can be ordered by mail from the publisher. Please include $1.50 for
postage. **But try your bookstore first!**

COURAGE BOOKS

An imprint of
Running Press Book Publishers
125 South 22nd Street
Philadelphia, Pennsylvania 19103

This Book Belongs To:

_____

♥

This book is dedicated to the memory of my mother

Looking Back

Happy scenes of childhood flood my memory and I am once again back home with my parents, laughing and being hugged by both of them. Hugging came easily in our home and while there were the usual moments of unhappiness and even anger, we seemed to spend a great deal of time just having fun.

My father loved model trains and the basement of our home was one vast miniature railroad with houses and trees and tiny people. He built the railroad and all the trains himself and as a child I spent many hours watching him work at his meticulous craft.

Mother loved cats—real ones and tiny porcelain and glass ones. She filled glass cases with them and they were always a perfect gift on any occasion. Mother died while this book was being written and I remember standing in front of one of the cabinets looking at those tiny crystal and china cats, so lovingly arranged, and recalling how each of them had marked some happier moment than this one.

If the depth of sorrow is a measure of the depth of happiness, then I was certain that my life had been filled with happiness. The source of happiness, the giver of hugs was gone and my father and I drew closer in our mutual loss.

I was born on June 12, 1932. My parents were childhood sweethearts, they married young and started a family. The depression changed their plans for a larger family and I, like my father, ended up an only child.

Before I was born, my mother's nickname had been Teddy but my arrival on the scene changed all that and she became Cee Cee because my cousin couldn't pronounce Theresa, her given name. So there we were—the three Teds.

Our days were filled with all the things that families contend with; laughter, confusion, and a naughty, mischievous little boy who needed to be spanked on certain occasions, not always as a celebration of his birthday.

Both of my parents loved flying and sailing; so we spent a great deal of time on the water and in the air. The big moment in a pilot's life is when, after months of training, he solos, which means going up alone.

When I went solo a few years ago after closing my New York based design firm, I called my new venture *Solobear*, for a bear who flies solo.

T. J. Solobear became my first alter ego/Teddy Bear persona. He did what I did and his travels were documented in a series of paper doll sheets. Visits to conventions and speaking engagements were occasions for him to get a new wardrobe on paper.

When I created *International Bearhugs*, a Teddy Bear club and newsletter, a new alter ego was created in the form of a Teddy Bear named HUG. Why, you ask, does this full-grown man need two alter egos? Because I am a Gemini!

I've been working (playing at work would be closer to the truth) since I was twelve years old. Mostly, like my parents, I enjoyed life as it was dished up and mostly it has been more feast than famine. I'm lucky, I guess.

Lucky, because I had a childhood that has never really ended. Lucky, because my friends know I'm really a bit nutty as well. Lucky, because I have a home full of Teddy Bears that help me make it through the day. They sit there patiently waiting to be hugged or photographed or asked their opinion on matters at hand. They are great friends and I love them all.

Of all the gifts my parents gave me; the gift of love and happiness, the sense of right and wrong, the respect for work, and the other gifts that parents bestow…of all the gifts, the *sense of wonder* was by far the greatest. ♥

MR. T.J. SOLOBEAR ATTENDS "BEAUTIES AND BEARS" LUNCHEON FEBRUARY 1982

T.J. LEAVES NEW YORK FOR THE FIRST MODERN DOLL CLUB OF NEW YORK LUNCHEON

DRAWN BY TED MENTEN

T.J. POSES FOR THE PHOTOGRAPHERS

T.J. SPEAKS ON A FAVORITE TOPIC

COPYRIGHT 1982 SOLOBEAR INC.

A TeddyBear Named HUG

Introducing the self-proclaimed Robert Redford of Teddy Bears, the spinner of yarns, the teenage idol, the perfect guest at any meal and the mastermind of many a honey heist…HUG!

A young bear with the heart and soul of a very wise and very old sage. He is filled with the wisdom of the ages, just like any other child. Only the very young are that wise!

A bear who knows his place, and if you don't set his place he'll set it for you. Opinionated on every subject and outspoken on every occasion, he describes himself as lovable but no wimp!

Introduce him to a baby and he'll dive under pillows shouting *HIBERNATE!* The same goes for dogs, dolls, and the man from UPS (who may be delivering a competitive bear). One of his quotable quotes is,"The better part of valor is retreat".

Here is a bear for all seasons, as long as that season has honey in it. Here is a bear who can never get enough attention, love or honey. Here is the great, heroic bear who is as flawless as he is faultless. Just ask him!

Welcome to The World According to HUG.

IT IS THE AMBITION OF TEDDYBEARS TO INSPIRE LOVE.

Why People Like TeddyBears

by Barbara Wolters, Editor of *The Teddy Tribune,* a publication about Teddy Bears.

Why are Teddy Bears so popular with people?

Teddy Bears are cute and adorable. Just look any Teddy in the eye and you will see that in spite of the wide variety of expressions among bears, the basic look is undeniably cute and adorable.

Teddy Bears make good companions. A Teddy will go with you anywhere… to the movies, to the beach, to bed, out to lunch, or anywhere you have in mind.

Teddy Bears are forgiving. A Teddy will forgive you, no matter what. He will still love you if you come home late from work, or leave the car windows open when it rains, or forget his birthday.

Teddy Bears are good listeners. You can tell your Teddy anything and he won't repeat it—not ever!

Teddy Bears are friendly. When you take your Teddy out somewhere, he will smile at everyone he sees. Most of the time, they will smile back.

Teddy Bears are tidy. A Teddy Bear will not throw his socks on the floor or leave dirty dishes in the sink. If he throws a party while you are gone, he will usually clean up before you get home.

Does all this sound like nonsense to you? Good! Nonsense is the *whole point* of Teddy Bears! Teddy Bears give us a chance to be silly. Silliness is a very important part of life. Being silly is just as beneficial and refreshing as meditation, exercise, or group therapy. And Teddys bring out our natural silliness. That's the *real reason* for their popularity—Teddy Bears are *fun!*

And this book is filled with ways you can have fun with your Teddy Bear!

Why TeddyBears Like People

by Dumper D. Dumper, Bear-in-Chief of *The Teddy Tribune,* a publication for Teddy Bears.

Why are people so popular with Teddy Bears?

People are cute and adorable. Just look any human in the eye and you will see that in spite of the variety of expressions among people, the basic look is undeniably cute and adorable.

People make good companions. People like to go places and usually they can be persuaded to take their Teddy along. Just don't ask for your own seat on the plane because that can get expensive.

People are forgiving. A human will forgive their Teddy, no matter what. But they will never forgive another human who laughs at their Teddy Bear!

People are good listeners. You can tell your human anything and he won't repeat it. He's not going to tell anyone anything he heard from a Teddy Bear!

People are friendly. People make friends easily, especially with people who are carrying Teddy Bears.

People are tidy. If you forget to straighten up after a party, they will usually clean up after you.

Does all this sound like nonsense to your Teddy Bears? Of course not! Nothing sounds silly to Teddy Bears! And that's why we get along so well with humans! They *never* look foolish to *us*!

Now read this book to your human and it will give you lots of ideas on how to make your lives together more *fun*!

I wish to express my thanks to the following people.
Daniel Flynn, my assistant and researcher.
Burton Stillman and the staff of Pulsar Graphics, who set the type.
The entire staff of Delilah Communications, especially Lanning Aldrich,
Richard Schatzberg and Richard Amdur, who guided me.
Iris Bell, who shared her love and knowledge of bears.
Barbara Wolters and 'Dumper', for their constant support and inspiration.
Nancy Olsen, for introducing me to so many wonderful bears.
Ed Sibbett, for patience and friendship.
Pat & Steve Gardner, Jan & Howard Foulke, Helen Nolan, Pat Nolan,
Irene Stasko, Yvonne Loehrer, Joyce & Les McClelland, Peggy Lewis,
and Dick Parsons for ideas and bears.

And very special thanks to Jeannie Sakol, for her enduring friendship
and faith in the project . . . a great big hug!

Contents

Introduction

In 1969, I was minding my own business and behaving myself in a bookstore when suddenly I was confronted by a book blatantly titled *The Teddy Bear Book*, authored by Peter Bull.

I was riveted to the spot and my heart was pounding so hard I thought there must be a parade nearby. I was sweating and my mouth certainly had gone dry. And in my brain formed the words I am not alone, there's another nut out there like me. It was rather like Robinson Crusoe finding his man Friday.

I remember that I was due at some business meeting or other; probably a minor function designed to change the world and the shape of things to come. You know, one of those meetings where life and death is decided and destinies are forever changed. And, if you are lucky, someone listens to you and you get a raise. Anyway, I never made it.

I bought the book, wandered up the street to Central Park and entered the world of arctophilia.

While my hold on reality had never been a strong one, and my grasp on the rudiments of adult behavior is slim at best, this wonderful book freed me forever of any pretense of normal adult behavior. I was out of the Teddy Bear closet!

Apparently, Mr. Bull's book had the same effect on millions of people around the world. In England, his homeland, Mr. Bull dreamed of a 'Gigantic Teddy Bear Rally.' On May 27, 1979, this event took place in England, at Longleat, the ancestral home of the Marquess and Marchioness of Bath.

On that momentous occasion, an estimated 50,000 Teddy Bears attended with the assistance of 20,000 human companions. The press was somewhat taken aback by the crowds and *Time* magazine ran the headline: "ARCTOPHILIA RUNS AMOK."

Meanwhile, back in America the Teddy Bear underground was out of the closets and into the streets. The Philadelphia zoo had record attendance at their Teddy Bear rally and all across America Teddy Bear lovers were having a party.

My life, never really normal in the first place, returned to a semblance of order and I stopped pretending that the Teddy Bear I was seen around town with really belonged to my niece who had wandered off.

And, like any other compulsive consumer, I began to adopt bears one at a time until pretty soon there was no place for humans to sit when they dropped by.

My good friend and fellow struggler in the worlds of

GRUMPY ED

♥

art and publishing, Iris Bell, sent me a copy of *The Teddy Tribune* and the rest (as they say) is history.

I wish that there was some profound, introspective, analytical thesis that I could espouse on the nature and behavior of arctophilists caught in their pursuit of the elusive Teddy. I even wish I could shed some light on the reason why we love our bears and find their companionship so delightful. But all that is rather like explaining what the Grand Canyon looks like as the first rays of dawn illuminate its walls…you have to be there.

Perhaps it is more like the story of the man embarassed by his behavior in some matter and his butler counsels him with the words, "don't bother to explain, sir, your friends don't need it and your enemies will choose not to believe you anyway."

Now, a few words about the nature of this book, why it was written and who I hope will read it.

I love my bears, and when I am good to them they love me back. Actually, they love me even when I'm not good because that is the nature of Teddy Bears.

While I certainly could be called a collector of bears (as well as dolls and books and all manner of stuffed critters), I did not want this book to be exclusively for collectors. I wanted this to be a book for anyone who loves their Teddy Bear.

One Teddy Bear, well loved, qualifies you as a genuine and certifiable Teddy Bear Lover. That's it.

A tiny memo about the terms in this book. The word TeddyBear, the words Teddy Bear and the word Teddys all refer to the same critter, a stuffed toy in the shape, more or less, of an animal called the bear. Usually, the resemblance ends there. Real bears are huge, often have bad breath and can knock your head off in one swipe. Even the cute baby bears we see tumbling about in the zoos could chew your arm off. Teddy Bears, on the other hand, simply love you all the time.

Most books spell the plural of Teddy Bears as Teddies; but as a Ted myself, I prefer to spell it Teddys—as in a gaggle of Teddys. My editor assured me that this liberty with the language, along with other infractions, was called the 'writer's style.' I'll buy that.

I guess I'll end this with one of those homespun yarns intended to endear the writer to his audience.

While doing research for this book in California, I was caught in the advanced grip of shopper's fever; attempting to buy out *The Ready Teddy*, one bear at a time—very quickly. The counter was stacked high with bears and the young lady behind the counter seemed to be taking the whole thing in her stride. Obviously she'd seen a bear nut before.

My best friend and fellow author, Ed Sibbett, was along for the ride, so to speak. Ed is a patient sort who endures my madness with a quiet smile of amusement. He is immune to shopper's fever and can actually browse.

As I frantically grabbed up bears, ostensibly to photograph for this book, Ed browsed.

On one shelf, sat a grayish long-haired bear with quite a grumpy expression. Ed picked him up and asked if I liked him. No I didn't, because he looked too grumpy and I wanted smiling bears for the book. Ed persisted that he thought this bear had presence. I replied that he liked the bear because it was grumpy like him.

Now Ed isn't really grumpy except if you accuse him of it…then he gets grumpy. Well, this bear became something of an issue with the result that Ed left the store and I had to carry all the bears home by myself.

It didn't end there. Ed insisted that the bear had liked me and was disappointed that I had left him behind. I replied that I still thought he was a grumpy-looking bear and that he would likely find a very nice home somewhere; and if he was so worried about the bear why didn't he adopt him?

It didn't end there either. Christmas came and sitting under the tree was a large box, elaborately wrapped, festooned with ribbons and punctured with air holes!

You guessed it! Inside was the grumpy bear bearing embossed army dog tags that read:

GRUMPY ED LOVES YOU

And if that doesn't tug at your heartstrings, nothing will. ♥

The Historical TeddyBear

In the year 1902 the Teddy Bear was born. This much everyone agrees on, but almost nothing else. Teddy Bears are named for the 26th president of the United States, Theodore Roosevelt. Again everyone agrees, even *Webster's New Collegiate Dictionary*, which defines Teddy Bear as:

> teddy bear ˈted-ē-, ted-ē-ˈ *n* [Teddy, nickname of Theodore Roosevelt †1919 26th president; fr. a cartoon depicting the president sparing the life of a bear cub while hunting]; a stuffed toy bear.

Well, that seems fairly straightforward and correct but wait, not everyone agrees that it was bear *cub*. Oh, boy, here comes the Controversy with a capital "C". And it's a big one!

Yes, the President did go hunting. In fact it was while he was in Mississippi to settle a boundary dispute between that state and Louisiana that he refused to shoot the bear in question.

One account tells of the hunter's frustration at not finding a single bear to hunt until finally a young bear cub was found and tied to a tree for the President to shoot. Reportedly, the President was angered by this unsportsmanlike idea and ordered the bear taken away, saying; "I draw the line. If I shot that little fellow I couldn't look my own boys in the face again."

In another version, the bear was a lean, black bear that had been chased by hunting dogs until it became exhausted. However, in a futile attempt to defend itself, the bear managed to kill one of the snapping hounds. At this point, one of the hunters managed to knock the bear unconscious with a blow to the head and it was tied to a tree for the President to shoot. In this account, the President is reported to have said; "Put it out of its misery" and the bear was killed with a hunting knife.

Adding to the confusion was the second key figure in

the controversy, the cartoonist, Clifford K. Berryman. His original cartoon, published on November 16, 1902 by *The Washington Post*, shows a full grown bear tied with a rope and the accompanying caption, "Drawing the Line in Mississippi." The cartoon refers to the boundary dispute as well as the President's refusal to shoot the bear. However, his most famous and best known cartoon (also dated 1902 and also having the caption "Drawing the Line in Mississippi") shows a young, shivering bear cub.

Berryman was one of the foremost political cartoonists of the period. After the great success of his original cartoon, Berryman used the bear (often referred to as Teddy's bear) as a kind of *signature* or *trademark* in his later drawings. There is no question that these cartoons contributed immeasurably to the overwhelming success of the toy Teddy Bear.

Another important contribution to the popularity of the Teddy Bear was the work of writer Seymour Eaton, who created *The Roosevelt Bears*. Named *Teddy B* and *Teddy G*, these bears appeared in both newspapers and storybooks.

While these bears were depicted dressed up and interacting with humans, they were real bears and not toy bears, i.e: Teddy Bears. The illustrations were done by either R. K. Culver or V. Floyd Campbell and the original books were published by Edward Stern & Company,

Philadelphia. Later reprints of these books are now available in paperback from Dover Publications, Inc., New York.

But the most difficult mystery of all to unravel is the question of who actually designed and manufactured the first toy Teddy Bear.

In 1903, the Ideal Toy Corporation of New York introduced its first Teddy Bear. The story goes that after Morris Michtom and his wife Rose created several toy bears for their shop he wrote to President Roosevelt requesting permission to name the bears after him. The President is said to have replied to the effect that he did not think his name would be of much worth in the bear cub business, but Ideal was welcome to use it. Thus the first Teddy Bear was born—or was it?

In that same year, 1903, the German toy maker Margarete Steiff created a toy bear at the request of her nephew, Richard.

Richard Steiff loved animals, and as an art student in Stuttgart, Germany he filled his sketchbooks with drawings of them. In 1897, at the Nill's Animal Show, he was fascinated by a family of young brown bears, and sketched them again and again.

At first the family resisted making the toy bear, but Richard's enthusiasm overcame their hesitation. But when the bear was shown at the Leipzig Fair in 1903, its reception was less than enthusiastic.

However, an American toy buyer from the George Borgfeldt Company in New York City felt that the toy bear had promise and ordered three thousand bears initially. A small beginning for the millions of Steiff bears that would follow.

Obviously, both companies had begun to work on their toy bear designs during 1902, but introduction of production bears into the marketplace seems to be consistently dated at 1903. By 1906 the Teddy Bear was declared a "craze" by *Playthings*, the official trade publication of the toy industry. In a long article published that year and titled, *The Plush Craze*, it was reported that one New York toy store reported sales of sixty thousand Teddy Bears.

While the Teddy Bear has remained a perennial favorite of children around the world since 1903, its popularity has accelerated during the past few years and seems to be on a steady rise.

The main concern of the manufacturers was that the supply of plush and mohair fabrics would run out and delay production. Since all Teddy Bears are essentially handmade, this meant employment for thousands of workers both in America and Germany. The Teddy Bear was a booming business and getting bigger every day. By 1908, sales of over one million were reported.

One can resist temptation but not a TeddyBear, he is irresistible.

The World According to HUG

Today there are many millions of Teddy Bears sold in America alone, and Teddy Bear Clubs have been formed by those who love and cherish them. While there may be some confusion about his origins, there is no question about his abiding and ever increasing popularity. ♥

HUG

HAPPY BIRTHDAY TO YOU, HAPPY BIRTHDAY TO YOU, HAPPY BIRTHDAY, MR. PRESIDENT!

Fun Makers for Little Tots

Set of 18 Round Cornered Blocks

Set contains eighteen 1¾-inch cubes. Two sides of each block have embossed letters. The other four sides have printed pictures and letters in colors. Shipping weight, per set, 2 pounds.
48 C 532—Per set.................48¢

Queen of the Stock Show with Stable Supplies

98¢

This beautiful Jersey stands so proudly because she's sure to win the blue ribbon at the Stock Show. She's all decorated for the occasion, too — white metal headgear, metal buckles, leatherette muzzle and imitation horns, bright glass lifelike eyes. The carefully moulded papier-mache body is covered with brown felt. Length, 6 inches. Mounted on metal wheels. The manger, wheelbarrow, milking stool, rake, shovel and blanket are included. **Imported.** Shipping weight, complete, 1½ pounds.
48 C 1145—Complete outfit.....................98¢

For Children's Story Books, see Page 422

A Great Big Christmas Stocking

Filled with 19 Surprises

Christmas never is complete without a stocking, so Santa has filled this great big roomy one with 19 fun-making toys — an armful of happiness for the younger child. If any toy illustrated in stocking is out of stock, another of equal or better value will be sent instead. Ship. wt., 3½ pounds.
448 C 3188—
Complete..$1.29

Small Size Contains 15 Toys

This stocking is just a wee bit smaller than the one listed above and contains 15 toys to delight the kiddies. If any toy shown in stocking is out of stock, another of equal or better value will be sent instead. Ship. wt. 2½ pounds.
48 C 3190....95¢

$1.78

Brightly Colored Wagon and Team of Horses—Hand Painted

This team is all ready to go to market for a cartload of supplies. It is such a fine team, too. Strongly made of wood, hand painted in gay colors. The horses are mounted on a wood platform with easy-running wheels. The cart is well nailed, brightly colored and resembles a real large truck. By attaching a cord, child may pull this toy along the floor. Complete length, 20 inches. Shipping weight, 3¼ pounds.
48 C 1108.................................$1.78

Durable Clothing for Children Is Shown on Pages 133 to 135

$1.19

A Fine Brown Horse with Stable Outfit

The body of this lifelike horse is well molded and covered with brown felt. He wears a complete imitation leather harness. Set includes an oat box, blanket, manger, wheelbarrow, shovel and rake. Length of horse, 7½ inches. Shipping weight, complete, 1½ pounds.
48 C 1146—Complete outfit..................$1.19

$1.39

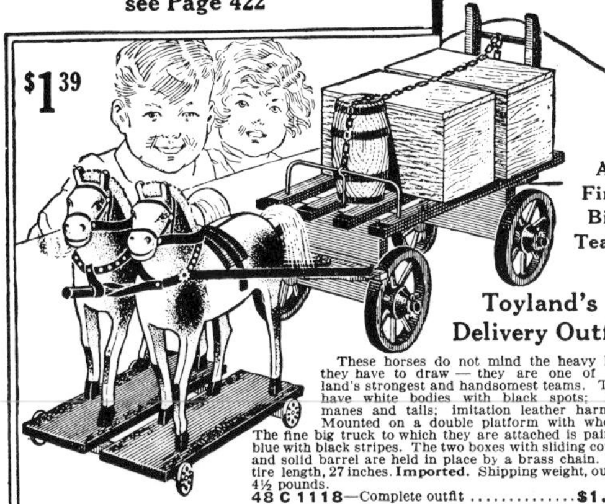

A Fine Big Team

Toyland's Delivery Outfit

These horses do not mind the heavy load they have to draw — they are one of toyland's strongest and handsomest teams. They have white bodies with black spots; hair manes and tails; imitation leather harness. Mounted on a double platform with wheels. The fine big truck to which they are attached is painted blue with black stripes. The two boxes with sliding covers and solid barrel are held in place by a brass chain. Entire length, 27 inches. **Imported.** Shipping weight, outfit, 4½ pounds.
48 C 1118—Complete outfit..............$1.39

Here They Are! The Jolly Teddy Bears

10 Inch Size 54¢

These jolly little Teddy Bears,
Who always love to play,
When hugged by little boys and girls
Will scare all gloom away.

These chubby bears are real pals. The more you hug them the more they squeal. The little 10-inch bear, however, is not quite big enough to have a voice, but he is just as nice as the larger bears. Their bodies are covered with cinnamon-colored plush, jointed at neck, shoulders and hips. All have lifelike glass eyes.

Baby Bear. Height, 10 inches. Shipping weight, ½ pounds.
48 C 3140..................................54¢
Mama Bear. Height, 14 inches. Shipping weight, 1 pound.
48 C 3147..................................89¢
Papa Bear. Height, 18 inches. Shipping weight, 1½ pounds.
48 C 3143................................$1.48
Grandpa Bear. Height, 22 inches. Shipping weight, 2 pounds.
48 C 3150................................$1.98

$1.19

Black Beauty

"Bow-Wow!" That's what he says when you push his tail down. He's such a lifelike little pal and always faithful. His fluffy coat of dog fur is black with white spots. Long bushy tail, realistic teeth, tongue and glass eyes. Length, 8 inches. **Imported.** Shipping weight, 1 pound.
48 C 3274.....................$1.19

He's a Mischief— But the Pet of Toyland

$2.39

So big and real, he's almost alive. Every child shouts with glee at sight of this fine bull-dog, with his large pudgy head, lifelike glass eyes and stump tail. His body is well formed of papier-mache, covered with felt in white with brown spots. He wears a leather collar and leash. Length, 15½ inches. Height, 11¼ inches. **Imported.** Shipping weight, 4 pounds.
48 C 3282.........$2.39

$1.19

Grunt, Grunt! Says This Pig

This good natured little piggy does not become angry and run away when you pull his tail. Oh, no. He likes to amuse children; so he nods his head, opens his mouth and grunts. Made of selected pigskin with composition snout, glass eyes and imitation teeth. Length, 10 inches. **Imported.** Shipping weight, 1¼ pounds.
48 C 3277.......................$1.19

98¢

A True to Life Kitten

Cries "Meow" When You Tease Her

Pull her tail, her mouth opens and she cries "M-e-o-w," just like a real live kitten. Has silky fur coat in black and white, natural looking ears and green glass eyes. Pink ribbon around neck. An exceptionally well made toy and a safe companion. It should last and amuse the child for a long time. **Imported.** Shipping weight, 1 pound.
48 C 3210.....................98¢

$1.29

Here's Bossy, the Cow

When you move her head from side to side she cries "Moo-Moo" like a real cow. Her body is well formed and covered with brown felt. Long tail. Mounted on a wood platform with wheels, so she may be pulled around the floor. Wears collar and bell. Length of cow, 12 inches. **Imported.** Shipping weight, 2 pounds.
48 C 3280...................$1.29

$1.19

Yes, He Is a Mule— But He Isn't Stubborn

He is mounted on a wood platform with easy running wheels and will roll along at your command. His body is well molded and covered with felt. Cries "Hee-Haw" when you duck his head. Length of mule, 11 inches. **Imported.** Shipping weight, 1¼ pounds.
48 C 3279..................$1.19

$1.39

Sheep with Real Wool

So nice and fluffy and woolly you'll just love to pet him. And he is as mild and gentle as a real sheep. He is 10 inches long and mounted on a platform with wheels, so you may pull him along the floor. When you nod his head he cries "Bah-bah" as if he were alive. **Imported.** Shipping weight, 1¼ pounds.
48 C 3281..................$1.39

Growling Bear

98¢

When you roll this playful bear over on his back, he growls — "Grrr-grrr." He is mounted on four wheels, so you may pull him along the floor by the chain. Imitation leather muzzle. Papier-mache body, covered with soft imitation bearskin in dark color. Length, 8¾ inches. **Imported.** Shipping weight, 1¾ pounds.
48 C 3276.......................98¢

Do Not Miss Our Wonderful Doll Display on Pages 402 to 405

In Praise of Older Bears

There is a great deal of discussion about antique bears and their value. Generally, the rule is that an antique is an object older than one hundred years. Since Teddy celebrated his eightieth birthday in 1983, he has not yet reached his antique majority. Perhaps he is better described as a *vintage* bear, like fine wine, aged with loving care. Or, as I prefer, an *experienced* bear! For surely nothing ages us like experience.

The question of a bear's value is, like anything else, a matter of personal opinion. What price beauty or love? It is my view that price is in the eye of the seller and value in the eye of the beholder. Still there are many collectors who, for reasons of insurance, wish to place a monetary value on their bears. For this purpose I recommend *The TeddyBear Catalog* by Peggy & Alan Bialosky. The original volume is filled with wonderful photographs and descriptions along with current prices. Also, this handy volume is full of history and helpful hints about Teddy Bears. The new, revised and updated edition was published in 1983 by *Workman Publishing Company, Inc.*

Experienced bears make wonderful friends as they possess all the knowledge and wisdom of the ages. Just looking at one of these old guys, his fur worn thin from loving hugs and his paws ragged from holding hands, takes you back along memory lane to simpler times now past; to childhood dreams and expectations.

Newer, *novice* bears, express the love of a child, while *experienced* bears convey the warmth and tenderness only age can bring. ♥

Dreams are the blueprints of reality.

The World According to HUG

*A man may wish
to bear his burdens
but he should never
burden his bears.*

The World According to HUG

*Self praise is like jam.
The thicker you spread it on,
the more sickeningly sweet
it becomes.*

The World According to HUG

The Modern TeddyBear

Modern Teddy Bears are not streamlined bears, but ones that are currently in mass production and available in stores.

If older bears are described as experienced, perhaps we should describe modern Teddy Bears as novice bears.

An experienced Teddy Bear brings with him a lifetime of knowledge and experience; the wisdom of silence and stillness in moments of great turmoil. The long-suffering patience that is learned when belonging to a child who is coming of age, and coping with the bewilderment that this period of time can bring, is what he does best.

The experienced bear has seen life through the heart and eyes of a child grown to adulthood and perhaps even accompanied that adult all the way to the end of the road.

The novice bear is just beginning life. Eyes all bright and innocent, fur clean and shining, paw pads clean and new, the novice is just at the start of life's journey.

And what an adventure it will be!

> *The young have so much to learn and so little time to do it in.*
>
> *The World According to HUG*

Today, all over the world, there are manufacturers of Teddy Bears producing all kinds of bears. The traditional Teddy Bears of yesterday are still being manufactured by *Steiff* and *Hermann* in Europe. In America, there are many exciting bears available from *California Stuffed Toys* as well as *Gund, Applause* and *Animal Fair*. *Steiff* has introduced several limited edition bears into the market, including the Richard Steiff bear that may have started the whole business in the first place.

The 1983 Richard Steiff bear is silver-gray with jet-black eyes and a charming expression. It is difficult to imagine that anyone could have resisted the original one if he looked at all like this charming replica.

In 1983, the marketplace was crowded with entries in the Teddy Bear race to fame and fortune. Speaking of fortunes, the elegant family of Vanderbears of *North American Bear Co.* is a charming family of bears dressed in black velvet outfits that are straight out of a Victorian fantasy.

Of course, 1983 also saw the introduction of the much heralded Care Bears. These pastel creatures are designed for mass appeal through mass marketing and appear on toys and greeting cards as well as T-shirts and pencil boxes.

In the Teddy Bear race for fame and fortune, as in any other race, there are winners and there are losers. Some of these new bears will get lost in the shuffle while others will find their way into the hearts of children of all ages.

The modern Teddy Bear, like his forefathers, is still the symbol of love and affection. It is the very nature of a Teddy Bear to be all things to all people.

He is the mirror of his owner's heart. He is a clean slate for them to write their dreams on. He is companion and conspirator in life's adventure.

And the novice bear is ready to begin the journey. He sits now on a shelf in a store somewhere...waiting on his new human companion to find him and to start his heart beating. ♥

North American Bear Co.

Joan Jaeckel Company

Steiff

California Stuffed Toys

A TeddyBear's virtue is that he cannot love himself ...only others.

The World According to HUG

Gund

Knickerbocker Toy Company

R. Dakin & Company

Hermann

Bears are well behaved because they don't know any better.

The World According to HUG

Applause

Eden Toys Inc.

Animal Fair

Man can be analyzed but TeddyBears ...simply adored.

The World According to HUG

North American Bear Co.

Happenings in Boutiques, Inc.

*If you would build castles
in the clouds,
it is best to stand
on a big rock.*

The World According to HUG

Dean's Childplay, Ltd.

Bear Haus

Applause

Kathe Kruse

*The best bears
go the best places
to be seen by the best bears
who have moved on.*

The World According to HUG

Russ Berrie

The Gentle Art of Handmade Bears

While it is true that in one sense all Teddy Bears are made by hand, since there is no master mold that creates them, the handmade bears shown here are really a form of art. These bears are not sewn up in a factory on endless rows of manned machines but rather are gently and individually created by loving and skilled hands.

Many of these creations are the work of one artist working alone and producing a one-of-a-kind piece of bear soft sculpture. In some cases these bears are the inspiration of a family working together to create another family of bears. And in the great tradition of Gilbert and Sullivan or Rodgers and Hart, a creative team works in concert to produce a single work of art.

Each artist has a vision and a point of view. Perhaps memories of childhood bears or bears from books or dreams feed their imagination and fire their creative energy. However it happens, the creative force produces a bear that is special and quite unique.

While every bear is unique and special to its final owner, these handmade guys start out special because they have been brought to life with caring and loving hands.

*Old age does not come
to the young at heart,
it only disguises them.*

The World According to HUG

In America, bear makers seem to prefer living in the Northwest and on the California coast. This may be because the Love Generation of the 1960s migrated west bringing with them their crafts and affection for handmade objects. Grown older, with children of their own, these artisans have turned to bear making. Certainly, the availability of handmade bears is greater in California than anywhere else in America.

But bear making is widespread across America and Canada and these beautifully crafted critters show up at almost every Craft Show, Church Bazaar, and County Fair.

It is said that secretly every person is an author and has at least one book in him. Not so secretly, people who love bears yearn to create one of their own. While patterns and kits abound through mail-order houses, they are someone else's dream bear.

So, if you want to create a bear of your own, just close your eyes and imagine him. If you're lucky he will come to you in a dream, take your hand and guide you through the creative process. More often than not, he will remain elusive, just out of reach to mere mortals. Like the *Book Muse* who speaks to writers, the *Bear Muse* touches a chosen few.

The artists whose bears appear here are but a few of the hundreds of people in the world who make bears by hand. They are a selection chosen to show the variety and versatility of their creators. ♥

Collee Bears

Graham Gridley Bear Co.

Bev Miller

Carrousel

Rita Maher

*TeddyBears don't dream,
but they are good
at watching dreamers.*

The World According to HUG

Lindsay / Purpus Bears

Doris King Originals

Beverly Port

A compliment, like a gift, is best wrapped simply.

The World According to HUG

Bearly There Co.

The Chocolate Bear

Bearly There Co.

*Nothing has real value
except as perceived by
the one who desires it.*

The World According to HUG

Ballard Baines Bear Co.

Collee Bears

Zücker Bears

A poet describes life not as it is, but as he would have it.

The World According to HUG

Kingery Co.

ARIZONA

Kenja Designs
Jane Carlson
139 W. Pershing Ave.
Phoenix, AZ 85029

Sal's Pals
Sarah McClellan
8622 E. Oak St.
Scottsdale, AZ 85257

Brandie Bear
Arla S. Conn
1601 N. Kelly Pl.
Tucson, AZ 85715

CALIFORNIA

Sea Bark Teddys
P.O. Box 2840
Alameda, CA 94501

Echoes of the Past
Lori Gardiner
30 S. First Ave., Suite 181
Arcadia, CA 91006

Printz Miniatures
Leta Robinson
530 Printz Rd.
Arroyo Grande, CA 93420

Frances Kampert
632 Alvarado Rd.
Berkeley, CA 94705

Darling Bears
Sue Darling
P.O. Box 3673
Big Bear Lake, CA 92315

Collee Bears
Colleen Tipton
1825 Forest Ave.
Carlsbad, CA 92008

Bear Buddy
P.O. Box 7225
Carmel, CA 93921

Beth Garcia
25673 Flanders Dr.
Carmel, CA 93923

Joanne Purpus, Ltd.
Joanne Purpus
579 La Costa Ave.
Leucadia, CA 92024

Veneta Smith
900 S. Rancho
Colton, CA 92324

Kubbies
Eleanor Ramsey
4375 Dina Ct.
Cypress, CA 90630

Zucker Bears
Barbara Sixby
P.O. Box 2475
Dublin, CA 94568

Beverly Port

Zora Galante
3616 Fashion Ave.
Long Beach, CA 90810

Maria Kwong Studio
3402 W. Olympic Blvd.
Los Angeles, CA 90019

Cynthia Josephs
P.O. Box 1245
Mendocino, CA 94560

The Chocolate Bear
Catherine Bordi
P.O. Box 7501
Menlo Park, CA 94025

Bob & Carol Raikes
P.O. Box 82
Mount Shasta, CA 96967

Jeanie Campbell
10215 Fair Oaks Blvd.
Fair Oaks, CA 95628

Bonnie Franklin Originals
Bonnie Franklin
2245 Currier Pl.
Fairfield, CA 94533

Flore's Bears
Flore Emory
P.O. Box 1888
Fallbrook, CA 92028

Sylvia Lyons
20437 Viewpoint Rd.
Castro Valley, CA 94546

Martex Bearly Bears
17540 Ventura Blvd.
Encino, CA 91316

Huggle Bear & Friends
21081 E. Milton Rd.
Linden, CA 95236

Shastabear
Pat & Alan Stewart
P.O. Box 384
Mount Shasta, CA 96067

Maureen Eckert
1615 Sycamore St.
Napa, CA 94558

Marilyn Van Auken
P.O. Box 7187
Imola, CA 94558

Georgie Bears
4642 Alta Rica Dr.
La Mesa, CA 92041

Roberta Viscusi
3009 Silverado Tr.
Napa, CA 94558

Whim C. Bears
1100 Raymond Ave.
Napa, CA 94558

Shirley Macone
1819 Dorrit St.
Newbury Park, CA 91320

Margory Hoya Novak
P.O. Box 1554
Novato, CA 94948

Elegant Fantasies
Cheryl Lindsay
1366 Eldean Ln.
Oceanside, CA 92054

The Strawberry Patch
Karen Haddon
142 Crestview Dr.
Orinda, CA 94563

Alleluia Bears
Susan Henderson
1844 Channing Ave.
Palo Alto, CA 94303

Bear Existence
Merilyn Alexander
P.O. Box 922
Pasadena, CA 91102

Susan Kruse
431 Wooden Dr.
Placentia, CA 92670

C.J. Bears
311 Orchard Ave.
Redwood City, CA 94061

Doris King Originals
Doris King
4553 Landolt Ave.
Sacramento, CA 95821

Kathy's Bear Hugs
3349 Romford Way
Sacramento, CA 95827

Flora's Teddys
Flora Mediate
190 Malcolm Dr.
Pasadena, CA 91105

Willie Bears
7628 Elm St.
San Bernardino, CA 92410

Schneider Bearworks
P.O. Box 112055
San Diego, CA 92111-0100

Heirlooms
Lynda Carswell
115 Genesee St.
San Francisco, CA 94112

Jean Kind
2165 15th Ave.
San Francisco, CA 94116

Elsa's Studio Gallery
97 Boston Ave., Suite 107
San Jose, CA 95128

Roley Bear Co.
792 S. Third St.
San Jose, CA 95112

Pat Temps
15 Fleming Ave.
San Jose, CA 95127

Brad Blakely
8316 E. Sheffield Rd.
San Gabriel, CA 91775

Judy Lewis
1128 Riviera Dr.
Santa Ana, CA 92706

Jo Ann Baise
178 Vista Del Mar
Santa Barbara, CA 94116

Bear Seasons
Joyce A. Baechtel
336 La Crosse Ave.
Santa Rosa, CA 95405

Heidibears
2369 Morrison Ln.
Suisun, CA 94585

Traditional Handcrafts
Suzanne De Pee
2208 S. Valley
Visalia, CA 93277

Wes Soderstrom
P.O. Box 60
Woodland Hills, CA 91365

Wright Designs
Beverly Martin Wright
890 Patrol Rd.
Woodside, CA 94062

Bearly There
Linda Speigel
14776 Moran St.
Westminster, CA 92683

Collee Bears

Gailloraine Originals
407 Brentwood Dr.
Tehachapi, CA 93561

Janet & Garret Sakamoto
P.O. Box 3182
Torrance, CA 90510

Animal Trax
1551 W. 13th, Suite 309
Upland, CA 91786

COLORADO

D.G. Enterprises
Diane Gard
1005 W. Oak St.
Fort Collins, CO 80521

Terol Reed
6563 S. Saulsbury Ct.
Littleton, CO 80123

CONNECTICUT

Adoptabear
16 Briarwood
Farmington, CT 06032

Baskets and Bears
Rev. Chester D. Freeman Jr.
44 Congress St., #302
Hartford, CT 06114

DELAWARE

Bar Harbor Bear Co.
P.O. Box 498
Bear, DE 19701

FLORIDA

Janna Joseph
P.O. Box 687
Dunedin, FL 33528

GEORGIA

Peach Promotions
21 Cantey Pl. NW
Atlanta, GA 30327

IDAHO

Barbie Adamson
412 First Ave.
Lewiston, ID 83501

INDIANA

The Teddy Bear Factory
Pat Ryder
7007 S. Ketcham Rd.
Bloomington, IN 47401

Liz Bruckman
12222 Castle Ct.
Carmel, IN 46032

Brick Street Bears
P.O. Box 362
Zionville, IN 46077

IOWA

J & P Enterprises
Box 3702
Des Moines, IA 50322

KENTUCKY

Bearly Suitable
Linda Groves
413 Sprite Rd.
Louisville, KY 40207

MAINE

Mountain Bear Manufacturing
P.O. Box 663
Bangor, ME 04401

Carol-Lynn Rossel Waugh
5 Morrill St.
Winthrop, ME 04364

MARYLAND

Bears by Cappi
Cappi Warnick
940 Lance Ave.
Baltimore, MD 21221

Sara Phillips
30 Locust St.   #2
Manchester, MD 21102

Pleasant Walk Folk
Joyce Sheets
11025 Pleasant Walk Rd.
Myersville, MD 21773

Dickie Harrison
239 Deep Dale Dr.
Timonium, MD 21093

MASSACHUSETTS

**Evergreen Farm
Wool Shop**
Oxford Dudley Rd.
Dudley, MA 01570

Barrington Bears
Elva Hughes
P.O. Box 192
Hinsdale, MA 01235

Nostalgia Nook
Maxine Look
115 Winthrop St.
Medford, MA 02155

April Whitcomb
3 Larspur Way   #3
Natick, MA 01760

Carole Bowling
P.O. Box 272
W. Roxbury, MA 02132

MICHIGAN

Carrousel
Terry & Doris Michaud
505 Broad St.
Chesaning, MI 48616

American Folk Bear Co.
27787 Forestbrook
Farmington Hills, MI 48018

MINNESOTA

Harry Bears
Valerie Volding Larson
10752 Cavell Rd.
Bloomington, MN 55438

The Bear Tender
Marlene Wendt
5935 Lyndale Ave.
Brooklyn Ctr., MN 55430

Kathy Nerison
1302 69th Ave. N.   #301
Brooklyn Ctr., MN 55430

Sue Goettl
P.O. Box 1
Eagle Lake, MN 56024

MISSOURI

Classic Creations
P.O. Box 3882
Springfield, MO 65808

Marilyn Quon
4720 Hanover Ave.
St. Louis, MO 63123

NEW JERSEY

Helen L. S. Ferguson
Route 3, Box 15
Califon, NJ 07830

Graham Gridley Bear Co.

Teddies by Sandy
Sandy Schultz
400 Stevens Rd.   #4012
Wallington, NJ 07057

HuBears
341 Westwood Dr.
Woodbury, NJ 08096

NEW YORK

Bears 'N Things
Dee Hockenberry
14191 Bacon Rd.
Albion, NY 14411

J. D. Babb Co.
Diane Babb
1266 Ivon Ave.
Endicott, NY 13760

**Hoke's Home of
Adoptable Bears**
315 Tamerack St.
Liverpool, NY 13088

Hilary King
P.O. Box 442
Flushing, NY 11367

Pleasant Visions
Janet Baty
307 N. Lowell Ave.
Syracuse, NY 13204

NEVADA

Lynn Lumley
3213 Pine Ln.
Carson City, NV 89701

Kyle Warner
349 Yosemite
Las Vegas, NV 89107

Nevada Bears
Eloise Page
14 Mason Rd.
Yerington, NV 89447

NORTH CAROLINA

Ann Tripp
507 Gatewood Ave.
High Point, NC 27260

Jackie O. Key
609 W. Lexington Ave.
High Point, NC 27262

OHIO

Ann's Bear Collection
Ann B. Peters
203 Union St.
Columbiana, OH 44408

Kathy Pridemore
3601 Sodom Rd.
Hamersville, OH 45130

Holly Dyer
203 Water St.
Mt. Blanchard, OH 45867

LaNore Kaplan
2983 Edgewood Rd.
Pepper Pike, OH 44124

Bearcrafts
Regina Brock
2621 Brady Lake Rd.
Ravenna, OH 44266

OKLAHOMA

Bearaphernalia
Lisa Schiller
5817 S. New Haven
Tulsa, OK 74135

OREGON

My Bears
Deanna Duvall
1405 Birch St.
Forest Grove, OR 97116

Maggie Anderson
502 NW Savage St.
Grants Pass, OR 07526

Teddy Bear Parade
Diane Marsh
P.O. Box 521
Hubbard, OR 97032

Lois Beck
10300 SE Champagne Ln.
Portland, OR 97266

Old Time Teddy Bears
Karen Walters
304 SE 87th Ave.
Portland, OR 97216

Woolly Bear & Co.
Lynda Carter
669 Evergreen St.
Stayton, OR 97383

Trickett's Teddy Trolls
Virginia Trickett
P.O. Box 1448
Tualatin, OR 97062

PENNSYLVANIA

Jody Battaglia
321 Brookwood Dr.
Downington, PA 17326

Bears by Nett
Gary Nett
601 Taneytown Rd.
Gettysburg, PA 17326

Bear'ers' With A Heart
124 Poplar Ave.
Hummelstown, PA 17036

The Bear Foot
Joyce Shaffer
35 W. Fourth St.
Lansdale, PA 19446

Truly Fine Bears
by Alessandra
P.O. Box 666
Whitehall, PA 18052

TENNESSEE

Barbara's Bearworks
Barbara Beckett
P.O. Box 795
Collegedale, TN 37315

Beckett Originals
Bob & June Beckett
Route 1, Box 141-1A
Deer Lodge, TN 37726

TEXAS

Trunkful O' Teddies
Theresa May
329 E. Garrett Run
Austin, TX 78753

Phebe Bears
Phebe Phillips
P.O. Box 2894
Dallas, TX 75205

Mereart
9851 Sagepike
Houston, TX 77089

Lynn Haney Designs
2317 17th St.
Lubbock, TX 79411

Marjorie Turner
801 Laurel Ln.
Nacodoches, TX 75961

UTAH

Fur Real
Gladys Logan
10050 Bell Canyon Cir.
Sandy, UT 84092

VERMONT

Handmade Teddy Bears
Elaine Leach
14 Elm St.
Brattleboro, VT 05301

Green Mountain
Teddy Bears
P.O. Box 85
South Ryegate, VT 05069

VIRGINIA

Grrr Designs
Gayle Wilson
3200 Porter St.
Richmond, VA 23225

WASHINGTON

Bear Mama
Joan Erdahl
P.O. Box 518
Belfair, WA 98528

Ballard Baines Bear Co.
1826 114th NE
Bellvue, WA 98007

Terry Bears
Terry Seim
P.O. Box 7943
Federal Way, WA 98003

Fairy Tale Bears
Pat Getchell
1055 Firpark Ln.
Fircrest, WA 98466

Candace
34714 NE 145th
Duvall, WA 98019

Graham Gridley Bear Co.
Mary Olsen
P.O. Box 264
Graham, WA 98338

Heartworks
Laura Schmitt
P.O. Box 354
Indianola, WA 98342

Holstad's Collectibles
23625 105th Pl. SE
Kent, WA 98031

Mary Lee O'Conner
1407 E. Chicago St.
Kent, WA 98031

Wainwright Bears
202 First St.
Langley, WA 98260

Luvin' Stuffins
Pat Morgan
P.O. Box 518
Lynnwood, WA 98046

Time Machine Teddies
Beverly Port
P.O. Box 711
Retsil, WA 98378

Bitsy Bears
Kimberlee Port
P.O. Box 632
Retsil, WA 98378

My Bear
Janie Comito
725 N. 98th
Seattle, WA 98103

Debartolo Originals
P.O. Box 33889
Seattle, WA 98155

Fey Originals
Michelle Temple
19226 12th NE
Seattle, WA 98155

Fujita-Gamble Teddies
Elaine Fujita-Gamble
19609 19th NE
Seattle, WA 98155

Bearly Beauties
Nadine Rushfeldt
7105 E. Roosevelt Ave.
Tacoma, WA 98404

WEST VIRGINIA

Fran Richards
174 Tartan Dr.
Follansbee, WV 26037

WISCONSIN

Rebecca Iverson
Route 1
Amery, WI 54001

Bears by Claire
Claire Marini
430 Lynnwood Ln.
Brookfield, WI 53005

Little Honey Bears
Linda Schmal
621 Rose St.
La Crosse, WI 54601

Tammies' Teddys
Tammie Lawrence
4562 N. 77th St.
Milwaukee, WI 53218

Loaded For Bear Co.
Nancy Hall
110 N. Main St.
Pardeeville, WI 53940

Ragtime Teddies
Jean Klipstein
Route 2
Rio, WI 53960

HUG says: Don't forget
to enclose a **SASE**.

Self
Addressed
Stamped
Envelope

*A good listener is
someone who can sleep
with his eyes open.*

The World According to HUG

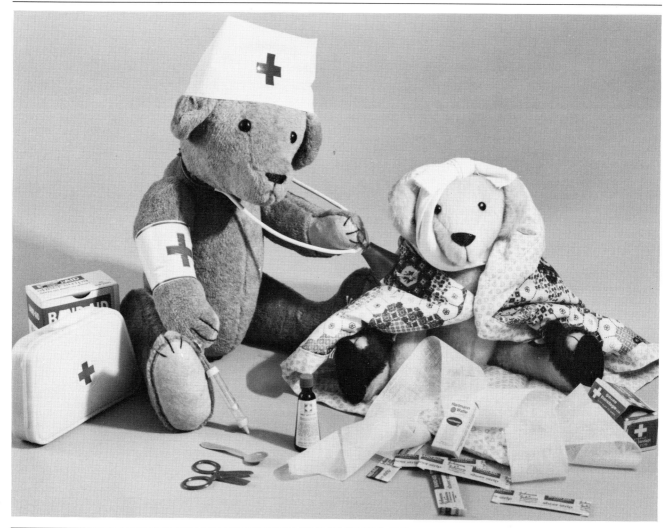

What to do When Teddy is Damaged

Often, in the course of human and Teddy Bear events, the bear suffers damage at the hands of a careless child or thoughtless parent. Patient and long-suffering, Teddy Bears endure this abuse with a loving smile and a kindly heart. And they have no memory of pain.

If one such tragedy should befall your bear, if he should lose an ear (his most vulnerable spot) or his paw pads become ragged and soiled, never fear, the Doctor is here!

If Teddy gets a rip or a split seam, sew him up with needle and thread. If the damage is extensive and there are holes to be filled or limbs to be replaced, get a matching piece of fabric and patch the area. Usually, one of the Teddy Bear supply houses will have a selection of fabrics that will do the trick.

If his eyes are missing you can use old shoe buttons or, once again, check the supply houses. His nose and mouth can be repaired with lightweight thread and even embroidery thread. Make sure that you use color-fast thread for this. If your bear is an old, experienced bear, be sure to repair him before you bathe him. You don't want the color bleeding all over his face.

A stitch in time saves nine... but a stitch in a bear saves stuffing.

The World According to HUG

If his ear has been torn off, pin it back in position and stitch it on. It is a good idea to baste the ear first, remove the pins and see if you like the way it sits on his head. Then go back and sew it down very securely. Many mothers with young children take the precaution of sewing the ears (even on new bears) just to be extra safe.

New paw pads are the most common repair that bears need. The felt gets soiled and torn and the bear starts to look threadbare and shabby. To replace paw pads, put the new pads over the old ones and use tiny stitches to secure them in place. Black or dark brown button or upholstery thread can be effectively used to define the bear's digits.

Just remember that a Teddy Bear is a cherished friend and should not be discarded because a little stuffing falls out. He has taken the time to love and comfort you or your child, now you must take the time to comfort and repair him. He will forget the pain but he will not forget you! ♥

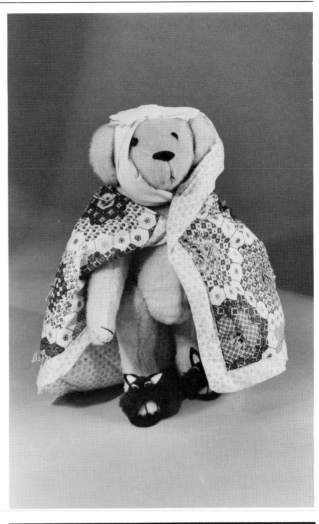

Any TeddyBear who is at all important should be hugged immediately.

The World According to HUG

HUG

HUG, WHERE IS MY TIE?

HUG, WHERE ARE MY CUFF LINKS?

HUG, WHO TIED MY SHOELACES TOGETHER?

MR. MISCHIEF STRIKES AGAIN!

TED MENTEN

How to Give Your TeddyBear a Bath

Since ancient times, men and women have enjoyed the pleasures of the bath. In Egypt, the land of the Pharaohs, perfumes and rare oils were part of the bathing process. During the Golden Age of Greece, poets and philosophers exchanged ideas while enjoying a steam bath, and the glorious Roman Empire built great public bathhouses that resembled the temples of the gods.

It is reported that Napoleon had twenty or more perfumes available after bathing. In all of history, bathing has been a glorious tradition, with the possible exception of boys like Huck Finn, who just hated the Saturday night ritual.

Today, the marketplace and TV offer an ever-increasing variety of products that clean and restore our bodies, hair, cars, floors, furniture and rugs. There are even special soaps and fancy perfumes for cats and dogs. The exotic chinchilla, for instance, requires a very special bath of *Fuller's Earth* to clean his luxuriant coat.

Unfortunately, there are no special bath products made exclusively for the Teddy Bear. So, we must improvise. Here are a few Helpful Hints for Teddy's first bath.

A well worn TeddyBear is a well loved TeddyBear.

The World According to HUG

While there are many considerations before you actually submerge Teddy into a tub of sweet-smelling foam, the most important concern is the age and condition of the bear.

The cleaning process for a modern bear is somewhat

easier than the process used to clean a vintage bear from the 1930s. Equally important is the actual condition of the bear. Is he whole or in need of repair? Never bathe a bear before you repair him. After you have checked him completely and have repaired the damage, gently brush him to remove any surface dirt. You might want to vacuum him with a small, portable type vacuum cleaner. An alternate method is to use a hair dryer full power on the cool setting while combing out the hair with a wide-tooth comb.

A word about combs and brushes. Always buy good combs and brushes that have smooth edges and firm but gentle bristles. Cheap combs and brushes have sharp edges that can cut the fur fibers of Teddy's coat and bring about premature baldness. Caution: never use a comb or brush that was used by a human because the oils from human hair cause a static reaction with the synthetic fibers of plush. This rule also applies to your real mohair bears, as mohair is a natural fiber and will cause the same reaction with the plush fibers. Just washing the combs and brushes doesn't seem to correct the problem, so get two sets if you have both kinds of bears.

One note about cleaning old bears. If your new friend and treasure came out of an attic or has been hibernating in the basement or other dingy places, he may have acquired a few, forgive my bluntness, bugs. Ugh…bugs! Don't be upset, it happens. Here is where an ounce of prevention is worthwhile. Take Teddy by the hand into a small room and sit him on plain paper. Close all the windows and set off a bug bomb. I prefer the *Black Flag Formula S Automatic Room Fogger*. The twin-pack has two small cans and does the job nicely. Spray the bear lightly and leave him in the room until the fogging is over. Follow product directions carefully for best results. Usually, I do a batch of bears together as it gives them some company during the cleansing process. Be sure to keep suspect bears in isolation before the treatment lest their little friends decide to visit your other bears.

And now for the bath! Unlike Huck Finn, Teddy loves a good cleaning especially after a romp in the fields with the kids or a midnight trip to the honey pot. Remember that he is patient and long-suffering where chores are concerned and so must you be. Usually Teddy only gets a few baths in a lifetime, unless he is a child's companion, in which case it may be as frequent as once a week. Pick a nice quiet day and you will both have a jolly good time.

Whether your bear is antique or modern, it is important to exercise extreme care when bathing him. *Gentle* is the key word during this process. Always test Teddy's coat for colorfastness. Choose a small, obscure area that won't show, like his bottom, to test for color stability. There is always a bit of risk involved when cleaning a stuffed critter, so *patience* and *caution* are two insurance policies you can take out to reduce the hazards.

Here are a few things that you will need; combs and brushes, several soft terrycloth towels, a sponge, washcloth and electric hairdryer.

Modern bears can easily be washed with a warm solution of *Woolite* (follow package directions). Sit Teddy on a towel and gently apply the foamy solution to him with a sponge, soft brush or washcloth.

Starting with the head, rub the foam into his fur but do not get him actually wet. Do one small area at a time to avoid soaking through to the stuffing. Avoid getting his paw pads wet if they are made of felt. Also avoid wetting the thread used to make his nose and mouth as these may not be colorfast.

Remove the foam with a damp washcloth. Rinse out the washcloth and repeat until all the soap has been removed. If the bear is very dirty, you may want to repeat the process. Remember, use only the foamy suds for cleaning and always use clear, clean water for the rinse.

Gently towel dry, then comb and dry with the hairdryer set on a warm setting. Some dryers come on a stand, leaving both of your hands free to work. Or you can strap the dryer, facing downward, to an ironing board or tabletop.

When combing out your bear, start with a comb that has wide-spaced teeth. After any snarls are eased out you can use a regular comb for finishing.

Antique bears can be cleaned with the same method or by another process that uses a chemical solution called *Formula 10*. This is essentially a rug and upholstery shampoo and is available at *Woolworths* or similar stores. The great advantage of this product is that it is

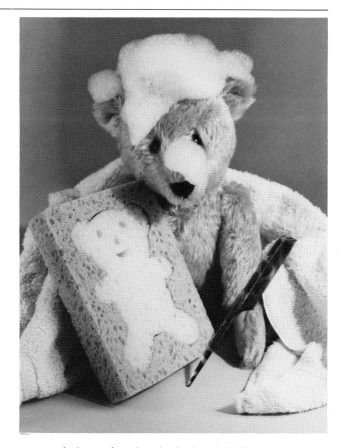

expressly formulated to do the kind of cleaning needed to get Teddy back into really tip-top shape. It is safe and odorless, as the package proclaims: "Formula 10 leaves no undesirable odors. Cannot turn rancid. Leaves material soft and fluffy with a natural feel and body." This is a quick, easy process that gets great results. Just follow the product directions. A 12-ounce box costs about $5, and will clean 480 square feet. That's a big bunch of clean Teddy Bears!

After Teddy has had a bath and been brushed out and combed, he is ready for a bright new bow and a trip somewhere special, like the ice cream shoppe for a honey freeze. And you, proud owner, deserve a pat on the back or a big hug from Teddy. ♥

HUG

The Well-Dressed TeddyBear

If clothes make the man, what makes the Teddy? Well, every Teddy loves a colorful bow, at least that's the case with all the Teddys I have ever known. Many bears enjoy hats and sweaters as well as jackets and dresses. Since Teddys seem to enjoy life in general, and a jolly time in particular, what could be more fun than dressing up? Just like little girls who slip into mommy's dress and high heels or little boys who put on dad's fedora and topcoat to act grown-up, Teddys enjoy the pretending that comes with a costume.

There is so much fantasy surrounding the life of a Teddy Bear and if you can't figure out exactly what will look best on your bear, try to imagine him as one of several characters in a play. Is he the hero or the villain, a courtier or a king, a prince or a clown? Is she a movie queen, a ballerina or a health nut jogger?

Older, experienced bears often look exquisite in period costume or in a cut down child's dress from grandma's old trunk. Kid's clothes, old or new, make splendid outfits for your bear.

Many Teddy Bears have established personalities like **Paddington** with his blue duffle coat or **Pooh** with his red sweater. But for the most part, bears come naked as the day they were born, all warm and huggable, ready to greet the new day and fill your life with joy.

Style is what you have, not what you wear.

The World According to HUG

Two fashionable bears that have distinguished themselves in the field of Teddy Bear Haute Couture are **Beau-Bear Brummel** and **Madame Coco** of Paris. Their fashion know-how appears in a monthly report from the fashion capitals of the world under the banner

When a Bow is not Enough. They have kindly consented to draw on their vast experience and share a few insights on the fashion scene. Gallant as ever, Beau-Bear introduces Madame as the first speaker. What follows is a human transcript of their views. Madame Coco speaks; "A lady is not (as some poets write) a work of art—which suggests a secondary form, that is, a thing created. But rather, a lady is, of herself, an art form. So, a lady IS art! Therefore, quite naturally it follows, a thing of beauty, an object of admiration. She is elegant in the simplest of bows, especially velvet or grosgrain or taffeta. Embroidered ribbons, so favored by French milliners, are best reserved for hats where their exquisite designs can be seen without being mangled in a knot.

"Since lady bears have lovely, luxurious fur, especially the fine mohair ones, it seems a pity to obscure that natural beauty with too much costume. *N'est-ce pas?* Understatement, *mes chères*, is the cornerstone of fashion. A hat with charming spring blossoms, a bow and a sweet smile are quite enough to be stunning. Perhaps a charming enameled heart-shaped pin or a string of pearls might accent the moment and express the personality. Lace shawls and collars, especially when held by an antique cameo pin are lovely for autumn and mild winters.

"Now, if one is fortunate enough to have inherited a child's frock or an old christening gown, I suggest that you reserve these for grand occasions, like Christmas or a birthday. Everyday fashion should be tasteful and therefore simple. The soul of fashion is in the heart and a Teddy Bear expresses his or her personality with *panache* and *élan*.

One cannot have a commanding presence with an unassuming past.

The World According to HUG

"One important note. Certain unfashionable bears, too overdressed and haughty, their noses held high and their bearing too assumed to be regal, might be advised to heed the fateful words of my grandmother (a bear of formidable splendor). 'If you would be placed on a pedestal, it would be well to remember that everyone below can look up your dress!' *Mon Dieu!*"

Well, that certainly is a provocative thought. Our next

If you want people to remember you, remember them first.

The World According to HUG

special quality. Clothes should maximize, not minimize personality and natural beauty. Thank you and have a good day."

commentator, Beau-Bear Brummel, has a few ideas of his own about fashion. Beau; "Nakedness is boring. You see one naked Teddy Bear you've seen them all. Get a tie. Get a scarf. Get a vest. Get dressed!

"It seems to me that a gentleman should have style and step out in his finest, be it designer jeans or a silk top hat. Show the world your stuff. Strut a little, show your colors. Be bright, wear red. Wear green. Wear multicolored stripes. Don't be blah!

"A gentleman bear might look his best in a white collar and black bow tie or a snappy vest with a watch pocket for his antique timepiece on a gold fob. A younger bear might prefer coveralls or a sweater. Hats really are an expression of personality and what bear does not possess personality? So, get a hat!

"The most important thing to remember about clothes for the Teddy Bear, male or female, is that they are intended to enhance, not obscure the bear's own

Thank you, Beau-Bear and Madame Coco for your very special insights into the ever-changing world of fashion.

On the more practical, less esoteric side of fashion, the following notes and comments may be of some help in selecting or making fashions for your Teddy Bear.

Generally, bears do a great deal of sitting about on beds and in chairs. When selecting an outfit, keep this in mind. Dresses that are open completely down the back are easier to sit in and the skirt will flare out nicely. Pinafores and jumpers are especially attractive for this reason. If you are buying an outfit originally designed for a doll, the best styles are those created for infant or toddler dolls as these tend to have high waistlines which are very flattering to bears. Since bears usually have heavy arms and broad shoulders, check to be sure that the sleeves of the outfit will fit over the arms. If your bear is a classic humpback type, this too, might cause a fitting problem.

Teddy Bears have short legs and high waists, so choose fashions that either enhance this quality or disguise it. Trousers and coveralls are a particular problem and most ready-made pants will need to be shortened.

Much of the fun of dressing up your Teddy Bear is the discovery of his versatility as a model. The changes in his personality as expressed by a simple bow or a hat or a full-length gown. If you have just one bear, you may want to indulge in a little unisex wardrobe as one friend of mine does with her bear who is aptly named *William or Mary Depending*. Depending on what he/she is wearing.

And so, as Beau-Bear Brummel says, "Get dressed! Don't be blah!" ♥

HUG

TeddyBear Paper Dolls

Almost as quickly as the plush Teddy Bear captured the hearts and imaginations of children around the world, the Teddy Bear as a paper doll became a favorite too.

In 1907, *The Boston Sunday Globe* ran a series of paper doll Teddy Bears with special outfits. The Behr-Manning Company advertised its sandpaper on a series of sheets featuring a bear called 'Barney.'

The popular Dolly Dingle paper dolls had one sheet called "Dolly Dingle's Friend Joey Goes to a Carnival." Published by *Pictorial Review* in 1924, the sheet depicts Joey with his carnival costumes, including one of a chubby brown Teddy Bear. *Pictorial Review* published several other sheets of Teddy Bears, including one called Ted E. Bear.

Many of the popular magazines of the early 1900s had paper doll sheets featuring children with their favorite toys, including the ever-popular Teddy Bear. Several of the Lettie Lane paper doll sheets have both dolls and bears worked into the art as accessories and props.

Queen Holden, one of America's greatest paper doll artists, created several Teddy Bear paper dolls, including a set of Christopher Robin & Winnie the Pooh.

The illusion of reality is reality.

The World According to HUG

Over the years since Teddy first debuted in stores and won the hearts of both children and adults, he has been the subject of paper doll art.

Teddy Bears dressed up in every manner of costume have been rendered by some of the most famous artists in America and around the world. Now, the Teddy Bear is an International Paper Doll Jet Setter! ♥

HUG

CHONEY

TeddyBear Dot-to-Dot

Connect the dots and color the picture.
(Solution on page 159)

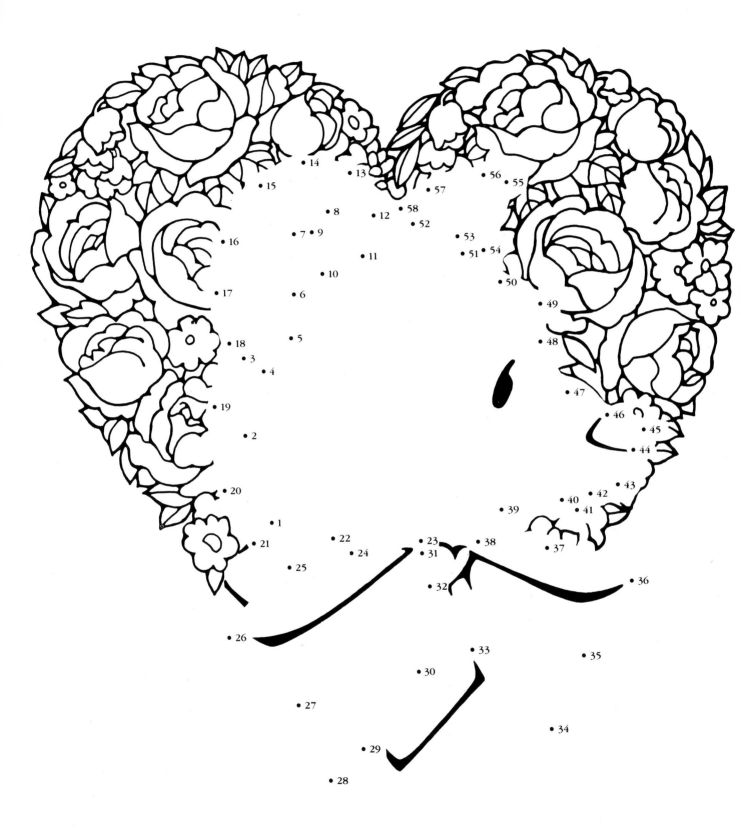

TeddyBear Puzzles

(Solutions on page 159)

This carpenter bear has two problems. A. Can you cut up this shape and reassemble it as a square. Use only two cuts!
B. Can you divide this square into six square pieces? Hint: They do not all have to be the same size.

Each Teddy Bear would like some land of his own. Can you divide this space, using only three straight lines?

Two of these Teddy Bears are twins. Can you find them?

How to Document Your TeddyBear

Oh the joy of a newborn bear! Proud mama or poppa that you are, you are now ready to document your new Teddy Bear (or your old one as the case may be). Bears love to "go on record" about all manner of things, especially themselves and their ancestors. Only ask a bear about his background and family tree if you are **a**) sick in bed with laryngitis and can't talk anyway, or **b**) have a long, lazy afternoon to waste with nothing more pressing to do than listen to your bear rave on about his Great-Uncle William the Unquenchable or his Great-Aunt Priss who sat on Teddy Roosevelt's lap at some function or other. Be warned, bears do go on!

Well, on to the documentation! First, remove the page with the birth certificate printed on it from this book. Now, make as many copies of the front and back as you need for all your bears. The back has the actual spaces provided for such pertinent information as the height and weight of the bear, his coloring and family connections. His religious and political views are his own and those questions are unconstitutional anyway. (The only party line that bears follow is the one that leads straight to the honey).

> *Just knowing that
> your Teddy Bear is home
> waiting at the day's end
> makes each day happier.*
>
> The World According to HUG

Take several photographs of Teddy for his special page in your documentation folio (you do have a folio, I presume). Choose one picture that captures all of his facial charms, his wistful glance, his clear eyes and his upturned smile. Choose another, full-length shot, to

Official

TeddyBear
Birth Certificate

Name of Bear

Name of Owner

Date of Adoption

PHOTO

PHOTO

TeddyBear Lovers Documentation Sheet

_____
Bear's Name

_____   _____   _____
Fur Color   Size   Eye Color

_____   _____   _____
Country of Origin   Age   Jointed or Unjointed

_____   _____
Bear Maker's Name   Where Purchased

General Description
_____

_____

_____
Date of Adoption

_____
Owner's Signature
_____
Price

ear. However, this is not the origin of the expression "Oh, stick it in your ear," although it may have been the inspiration for the button. But, I digress.

If beauty is in the eyes of the beholder, every bear will find a home.

The World According to HUG

show to the authorities if he should wander off in search of honey and require assistance finding his way back home again.

Measure him from top to bottom unless he is a bear in a sailor suit in which case you may measure him from stem to stern. No matter the method, get the facts.

Remember that there is a great deal of controversy over the question of tag removal. Some people (and some bears as well) think of those little gold buttons as an earring and insist on leaving them in the bear's

Personally, I remove the buttons and all other tags because a wise old bear once told me that bears never feel they have a permanent home until all tags and buttons have been removed, thus guaranteeing that they can't be sold or shipped away. ♥

HUG

HUG IS A VERY TALENTED BEAR.

REALLY, WHAT IS HIS TALENT?

HE CAN MAKE ME FEEL LOVED.

AH, SUCCESS IS SO SWEET!

TED MENTEN

Here is a design that you can color.

Here is a design that you can color.

How to Photograph Your Teddy Bear

Before you actually snap the first picture of Teddy, there are a few simple steps you can take to make sure every picture will be what you intended it to be.

The first thing to consider is the matter of focus and depth of field. Depth of field refers to that part of the photograph that is in sharp focus. The depth of field is controlled by the *f* number or what is often referred to as the *f* stop. The basic rule is, the lower the *f* stop number, the shorter the depth of field.

Another important thing to remember is that the depth of field extends both in front of, and behind, the area that you have pulled focus on.

For example, if you are shooting a sitting Teddy, his feet extend forward from his body. If you pull focus on his eyes, his toes may be out of focus. But, if you pull focus on the tip of his nose, which is a point about halfway between his feet and the back of his head, the whole bear will be in sharp focus.

Another equally important consideration is lighting. The drama and storytelling quality of a photograph can be enchanced or destroyed by the lighting design.

If you are shooting indoors, and have only one light source, either natural or artificial, you can bounce a bit of light off of a white board or a mirror or even a foil covered board. Reflected light gives a softening effect and cuts down on dark shadows.

If you cannot fail, you cannot succeed.

The World According to HUG

If you are shooting outside, a bounce board or some other reflector will help to soften the dark shadows caused by bright sunlight.

Unless you are shooting a passport photo of Teddy,

the best pictures tell a bit of a story and add some romance to the picture. This is where wardrobe and props can come in handy. A bright bow, some flowers, a sweater or hat add to the effect and drama of the picture.

Finally, a word about film. There are a great number of film speeds available on the market today. Remember that the faster the film, the more grain it will have.

For sharp, clear pictures, choose a film speed that will have a lower number. This is called the ASA number and is marked on the box. ASA 25 will naturally be slower than ASA 200.

Well, Teddy is dressed and waiting. The lighting is set in place, the film selected and the depth of field determined. Now, all you need is a little imagination and soon you will have an album full of pictures. ♥

Figure A. The bride bear photographed against a background of seamless paper.

Figure B. The bride bear photographed against a photographic background.

Figure 1. Teddy Bear photographed with equal left and right lighting.

Figure 2. Teddy Bear photographed with light on right side and foil reflector on the left.

Figure 3. Teddy Bear photographed with light on right side and white board reflector on the left.

Figure 4. Teddy Bear photographed with light forward on right side and slightly back on the left.

Figure 5. Teddy Bear photographed against printed gift wrap paper. Light on right with foil reflector on the left.

Figure 6. Teddy Bear photographed against black seamless paper with equal left and right lighting.

Figure 7. Teddy Bear photographed with prop butterfly. Light on the right with foil reflector on the left.

Figure 8. Teddy Bear photographed with hat. Light on the right with foil reflector on the left.

Figure 9. Teddy Bear photographed with coffee and cookie. Light on the right with foil reflector on the left.

Figure 1

Figure 2

Figure 3

Figure 4

Figure 5

Figure 6

Figure 7

Figure 8

Figure 9

What to Name Your TeddyBear

O h, the dilemma of choosing a name for your bear. Is he a boy or is she a girl? Or perhaps nothing so definite as that…something more elusive, mystical or spiritual, like a cupid or an angel, who are said to have no special gender.

Perhaps he is a Teddy, an Edward or even a Sidney. After all, he is who you want him to be, for he is yours to name. I am very fond of naming bears, all of my bears have names although I often misplace them (the names, not the bears) in my memory banks. I fear time has clouded my once crystal clear recall. However, the naming process is great good fun and I indulge myself in it as often as possible, which means finding new bears to name. A tricky excuse for a bear hunt!

The names come to me in different ways, but this little story illustrates a typical adventure in naming. While bear hunting in Cornwall Bridge, Connecticut, I dropped by *The Brass Bugle,* a charming barn filled with antiques. My friends Louise and Bob run the place and they have a sharp eye for really fine old goodies.

Well, they had this wonderful bear, hardly an antique, but really charming. So I bought him.

> ## *If a TeddyBear is worth having, he is worth buying.*
>
> *The World According to HUG*

As we all said our good-byes, Louise asked me what I intended to name the bear and I replied that I hadn't a clue. She suggested that I name it after one of them and I promised to consider the idea.

Driving toward home, I thought about their names. The idea of calling this very amusing bear, whose eyes are lower than his nose, simply Bob or Louise, was out of the question. Still, I liked the idea of naming this critter after my friends. Maybe Bobby or Louie would do. No, too simple. Then I thought of Bobby Louise and for a brief moment I thought I had it, but looking into the back seat at this sturdy little bear I knew that he was no Bobby. Almost disheartened, I suddenly hit on the perfect name. I would call him **Robert-Louise!** It has a nice formal ring to it, but is also just a bit nutty, like having your eyes lower than your nose.

What follows is a whimsical journey into the endless possibilities of naming your bear.

Are you musically inclined? Is your bear? How about **Andante** for a moderately slow bear or **Arpeggio** for a quicker one. Something more modern? Try **Babaloo**, **Bebop** or **Bongo**. A bear with fantastic style might be called **Capriccioso** or a plucky bear called **Pizzicato**.

You say your bear has personality? Try **Charisma**; charming, try **Elan**; puzzling, **Conundrum**; elusive, **Enigma**. Of course, there is **Cuddles** and **Dandy**, **Feisty**, **Fiasco** and **Fidget**. Maybe he's a **Hobo** or an **Isadorable**. Fast on his feet, **Lickety-Split**. Lazy as a **Lollygog** or fussy

as **Persnickety**. **Nuzzles** is a cuddler and **Me-Too** tags along. **Quandary** has a question that **Dinky** is too small to answer.

There are the twins: **Chow Mein & Lo Mein**, **Gucci & Pucci**, **Whatchamacallit & Thingamajig**. The triplets: **Faith**, **Hope & Charity**; **Athos**, **Parthos & Aramis**; and from the opera, *Turandot*; **Ping**, **Pang & Pong**. Here come the smallest bears; **Half-Pint** and **Munchkin** followed by that elegant number **Splendiferous** and the largest bear of all, **Behemoth**!

Many bears are bluebloods and to the manner born. Therefore called **Prince** or **Baron** or **Lord** or **Sir**. The ladies being **Countess**, **Duchess** or **Empress** or simply **Milady**. Since Teddy was named for one President, how about a quiet bear named **Calvin**. Or a revolutionary bear called **Robespierre** sitting across from **Talleyrand**. And who could forget a bear named **Lloyd George**?

Love is like a balloon.
It gives you a big lift.

The World According to HUG

Having fun? Meet a honey bear called **Ambrosia**. A dark molasses bear called **Baba au Rhum** with two friends named **Macaroon** and **Melba**. And who could ever forget that Italian diplomat; **Lord Mozzarella** and his dandy sidekick the **Parmesan Prince**.

A French Bear named **Beau Geste** or **Bonheur** for luck. A Russian bear called **Babushka**. An Italian bear might be named **Ben Trovato** meaning happily discovered or **Bellissimo** for beautiful. A Hindu lady bear, **Bibi**, and her bandit friend **Dakoo**. The Latin word for happy fault, **Felix Culpa** and his apologetic friend **Mea Culpa**. **Bubeleh** is Yiddish for darling while **Chutzpa** describes a perky but impudent bear, and the craziest bear of all is called **Mishugah**. Greek bears are **Callestra** for most beautiful or **Basilidon** if he has a regal bearing. Spanish bears may be called **Amigo** for friend and **Bandido** if they steal honey. Finally, the bears of Ireland are called **Mavourneen** if they are darling and **Boyo** if they are a wee lad.

The world is a circus with too few clowns.

The World According to HUG

Perhaps your bear's fondness for honey would cause you to call him **Baklava**, for the Greek pastry.

Like wizards and magic? Try **Abracadabra** or **Merlin**, **Jinx**, **Pixie**, or my favorite—**Pooka**, an Irish evil spirit.

Several of my more expensive bears have financial names like **Conglomerate** and **Collateral**. There's **Blue Chip** and **Fannie Mae**, **Moola** and **Megabucks** and off by himself, pondering noninterference, **Laissez-Faire**, the economist of the bunch.

Here's a potpourri of nonsense names that just makes me chuckle especially when I think about a bear with a surprising moniker like **Serendipity**. So hats off to; **Fig Newton**, **Flubbernutter**, **Hokey Pokey**, **Goober** and **Whizbang**. Smiles to: **Fauntleroy**, and **Marzipan**, **Wigglesworth** and **Tapioca** (and her cousin **Carioca**). Here's **Ignatz** and **Magoo**, **Wimpy** and **Walla Walla**, **Hootchie Cootchie**, **Hully-Gully** and **Bossanova**.

Many Foreign words have a nice flair and a certain *je ne sais quoi. N'est-ce pas?*

Last, but certainly not least, here are the words for *bear* or *Teddy Bear* in several languages:

Danish; bjørn (*bear*) Teddybjørn (*Teddy Bear*). Dutch; beer (*bear*) Pluchen beer or Teddy beer or beertje (*Teddy Bear*). French; ours (*bear*) nounours (Teddy *bear*). German; bär (*bear*) Teddybär (*Teddy Bear*). Hebrew; Dov (*bear*) Dubon (Teddy *bear*). Irish; mathgamain (*bear*) Béirín (*Teddy Bear*). Italian; orso

(*bear*) **orsacchiotto di pezza** (*Teddy Bear*). Norwegian;
bjørn, Teddybjørn (*Teddy Bear*). Polish; **Niedźwiedź**
(*bear*) **mis** or **zabawka** (*Teddy Bear*). Portugese; **urso**
(*bear*) **ursihno** (*Teddy Bear*). Roumanian; **urs** (*bear*)
ursultet (*Teddy Bear*). Russian; **medved** (*bear*)
medvazhanok or **igrushka** (*Teddy Bear*). Spanish; **oso**
(*bear*) **osito de trapo** (*Teddy Bear*). Swahili; **dubu**
(*bear*) **dubu** (*Teddy Bear*). Swedish; **bjorn** (*bear*)
Teddy björn or **leksaksbjörn** (*Teddy Bear*). Hungarian;
medve (*bear*) **játékmackó** (*Teddy Bear*). ♥

HUG

HUG, I'M BRINGING HOME A BEAR NAMED WENDEL.

HMMM... WENDEL THE WIMP.

WENDEL, THE WISP!

WENDEL WON FIRST PRIZE IN THE BIG BEAR CONTEST!

OH, WENDEL THE WINNER!

TED MENTEN

A Horoscope for Teddy

Casting a horoscope for your Teddy Bear is really a matter of personal choice. There are those who choose to cast it from the moment of birth, like humans, but when is a Teddy born? If you are a bear maker and are so inclined, you could start the bear's life cycle with the moment of your final stitch. But, what of all the Teddys not so well documented? Those purchased in a store and manufactured by a company far across the sea? Surely there is a simpler way and happily there is.

In doing research for this chapter I was directed to visit an old and very wise Teddy who lived with an even wiser and older person, an astrologer herself. The astrologer and the bear (named **Ursa Beara**) shared the secret of how to cast a perfect horoscope for a Teddy.

"Since birth begins with life or vice versa, we must set a standard for when a Teddy first comes to life and that answer is remarkably simple…a Teddy Bear first comes to life in the heart of the person who loves him. So, a Teddy is *born* the moment he is loved. Now, isn't that simple?" said Ursa Beara.

A TeddyBear's true beauty is in being lovable.

The World According to HUG

Having determined that the first time you saw your Teddy and loved him was (for example) on February the 4th, you would consult the charts and find that he is an Aquarian, born under the sign of Aquarius. Human horoscopes are very complicated to cast and humans tend to have many influences that alter and modify their personality but bears are very basic. It is fairly clear that while all bears born under the same sign are not alike, they are much more alike than humans born under the same sign.

Ursa Beara made several remarks about the differences and similarities of bears born under various signs, but the most telling, the most profound, was this: "There are no two bears alike because there are no two human hearts that are alike. And while it is true that all Teddy Bears love honey, *how* they love honey is determined by their Zodiac sign."

The mysteries of the universe have been pondered by man since the dawn of time. The Egyptians believed in astrology, the study of the stars, and since that time almost all men have turned to the heavens in search of some answers about their destiny.

Astrologers, working with a system of star charts, mathematically determine the direction and movement of the stars and planets to cast a Horoscope or personal star chart. The art of astrology is in the interpretation of the charts and no two astrologers seem to cast the same destiny from the same charts. Some people scoff at astrology as hocus-pocus or witchcraft; others think it is a real science. No matter. With regard to Teddy Bears, it is simply fun and a good adventure into knowing your bear a little better. ♥

ARIES
The Ram
March 22 through April 20

**The sign of the Warrior or Pioneer
Fire Sign
Ruler: Mars
Gems: Amethyst, Diamond
Color: Red · Metal: Copper
Compatible Signs: Sagittarius, Leo**
♥

Going on a secret mission? Traveling to a foreign country? Take a bear born under the sign of Aries. Enterprising and full of courage, these bears will climb the highest mountain and dive to the deepest depths. Adventure is the Aries bear's middle name. Straightforward and often pugnacious, his quick temper has its drawbacks. But if the honey is high up on a shelf, he will stack up boxes and chairs until he reaches the top, and he'll never look back. This bear is a born problem solver and maybe a born problem maker as well. Born under the sign of the Ram, this fellow will buck all the odds to come up a winner. ★

TAURUS
The Bull
April 21 through May 21

**The sign of the Builder or Producer
Earth Sign
Ruler: Venus
Gems: Moss-Agate, Sapphire
Colors: Blue and Pink · Metal: Copper
Compatible Signs: Capricorn, Virgo, Cancer**
♥

The Taurus bear will want to 'belong' to a permanent scene. To this end he will present a solid, steady, reliable front to the world around him. These bears born under the sign of the Bull can be determined, strong-willed, affectionate, trustworthy and often self-indulgent. The Taurus bear will stubbornly guard his honey and often appear greedy as he sits in an elegant chair and uses a silver spoon to devour the whole potful. And while he can be very charming, he is not to be rushed. But if you need some honey for a rainy day, he is sure to be the one who has it, for these bears are always prepared. ★

GEMINI
The Twins
May 22 through June 22

The sign of the Artist or Inventor
Air Sign
Ruler: Mercury
Gems: Beryl, Aquamarine
Color: Yellow · Metal: Quicksilver
Compatible Signs: Aquarius, Libra

♥

The Gemini bear is clever and witty on the one hand and changeable and restless on the other. This is the sign of the twins and often these bears appear two-faced, as they seem to be offering you their honey and taking it back at the same time. Talkative and amusing in conversation, they have a real flair for writing. And, no one can insult you with more flair than a Gemini bear. Always up-to-date and beaming with a childlike smile, these guys could be 80 years old and not look a day over 40. If you are short of honey, take this bear to the store with you and watch him con the owner with his smile. The Gemini bear is a born charmer. ★

CANCER
The Crab
June 23 through July 23

The sign of the Prophet or Teacher
Water Sign
Ruler: the Moon
Gems: Moss-Agate, Emerald
Color: Green · Metal: Silver
Compatible Signs: Pisces, Scorpio, Taurus

♥

This bear always wants to stay home and rearrange the furniture. Kindly and sympathetic, the Cancer bear possesses a powerful imagination that may lead to trouble. Gentle with the smaller bears and parental in the distribution and sharing of the honey, this sweetheart is often easily flattered and a sucker for the con artist. Often willing to listen to the tales and woes of others, he may suddenly become ill-tempered and moody. Often cautious with money and a born bargain hunter, he will watch the budget like it was the national debt. And if there is a coupon for free honey, he'll find it faster than any other bear. ★

VIRGO
The Virgin
August 24 through September 23

The sign of the Craftsman or Critic
Earth Sign
Ruler: Mercury
Gems: Pink Jasper, Sardonyx
Colors: Gray or Navy Blue · Metal: Quicksilver
Compatible Signs: Capricorn, Taurus

♥

Here is the Virgo bear, discriminating, modest, tidy and often just plain fussy. Finicky about the honey being pure and the datenut bread fresh, Virgo, for all his elusive beauty, can be a pain in the neck. Hard working, with a great appetite for both life and expensive honey, the Virgo bear at his best is eager to help his fellows. These bears have a marvelous sense of detail and are creative to perfection. Ask this bear to make a shopping list and it will be neat and well-organized with great attention to detail. But don't ask him to do the shopping…that could take forever. Often interested in hygiene, the Virgo bear loves a bath. ★

LEO
The Lion
July 24 through August 23

The sign of the King or President
Fire Sign
Ruler: the Sun
Gems: Ruby, Diamond
Color: Orange · Metal: Gold
Compatible Signs: Sagittarius, Aries

♥

Imagine a bear with a lion's mane and a lion's roar; that's the Leo bear. As the lion is king of the jungle, this bear is master of all he surveys. Magnanimous and generous, creative and a great organizer, he can be a bit of a bully. Hide your honey, here comes the boss. If there is a red velvet ribbon around he will find it and wear it. If there are gold tassels too, he'll wear those as well for this is a bear with a sense of drama. At their best, Leo bears are affectionate, optimistic and cheerful. At their worst, snobbish. Do not offer this guy a discount brand honey, he'll bite your head off. But be careful, his feelings are easily hurt. ★

LIBRA
The Balance
September 24 through October 23

The sign of the Statesman or Manager
Air Sign
Ruler: Venus
Gems: Diamond, Sapphire
Color: Indigo Blue · Metal: Copper
Compatible Signs: Aquarius, Gemini

♥

Two bears fighting? Sit a Libra bear between them, for harmony is this bear's middle name. The sign of the scales or balance makes this bear a peacemaker or a matchmaker. Romantic and idealistic, the Libra bear believes that there will always be honey and hugs for all. Often frivolous, discarding one bright bow for another, the Libra can be a devil of a flirt. Often sulking over imagined slights, the Libra bear may be the only bear to try to divorce you if you fail to show enough affection or keep the honey warm. And fellows watch out, a lady Libra can wrap you right around her little finger. Come to think of it, so can the gentlemen. ★

SCORPIO
The Scorpion
October 24 through November 22

The sign of the Governor or Inspector
Water Sign
Ruler: Mars
Gems: Topaz, Malachite
Color: Deep Red · Metal: Iron
Compatible Signs: Cancer, Pisces

♥

Beware of the Scorpio bear! Jealous, stubborn and resentful when crossed, this fellow is full of passion and fire. This is no bear to be taken lightly. Filled with purpose, this fellow loves, works and plays with an intensity that burns. The Scorpio is highly imaginative, discerning, subtle and determined—in all things. No mountain is too high to climb, no task beyond his dreams. The glow in his eyes will tell you that this guy is on the move, so watch out. He will jealously guard his honey and hide it away; and just when you have decided that he is selfish, he will share it with all. The Scorpio will usually over-indulge himself in work and play. ★

CAPRICORN
The Goat
December 23 through January 19

The sign of the Priest, Ambassador, or Scientist
Earth Sign
Ruler: Saturn
Gems: White Onyx, Moonstone
Color: Dark Green · Metal: Lead
Compatible Signs: Taurus, Virgo, Libra

♥

Capricorns are ambitious, always looking out for a good deal and promoting another bowl of milk and honey. Determined and disciplined, they are good generals and natural leaders. The Capricorn bear may spend a bit too much time keeping up with the Jones' bears, and tends to wear the latest designer jeans. But he does have a good sense of humor and can even laugh at himself. Give this bear a task and he will get it done but don't ask him to compete...competition makes him grumpy as a goat. As to the matter of honey—this bear will check his neighbor's brand and one-up him with a better brand. ★

SAGITTARIUS
The Archer
November 23 through December 22

The sign of the Sage or Counselor
Fire Sign
Ruler: Jupiter
Gems: Topaz, Turquoise
Color: Purple · Metal: Tin
Compatible Signs: Aries, Leo

♥

Oh, boy... here comes the optimist! Jovial, freedom loving, open-minded and a bit tactless, the Sagittarius bear is just plain good fun to be around. Life in the fast lane is his motto. Red cars, bright stars and Golden Blossom Honey for all! Don't let him run for office; he'll win. Unexpected is the word underlying his every mood. You say this is a formal occasion...he wears sneakers. You say you're sad...he'll stand on his head just to make you smile. But don't ask him how he thinks you look today because he'll really tell you. Whoops, there he goes in a big red car with a big bright star. ★

AQUARIUS
The Waterbearer
January 20 through February 19

The sign of the Truth-Seeker or Scientist
Air Sign
Ruler: Uranus
Gems: Sapphire, Amethyst
Color: Electric Blue · Metal: Uranium
Compatible Signs: Libra, Gemini, Aries

♥

See this old bear, standing quietly at attention by his friend as life goes by on parade, he is an Aquarian. Faithful and loyal to a fault, these imaginative, creative bears have a positive outlook on life that is a joy. While an Aquarian can be unconventional, even eccentric at times, he is just flexing his personality, trying out a new mode of expression. He can be high up on a hill watching a sunset but one cry for help will bring him on the run with the words 'can I help' already on his lips. The Aquarius bear may seem reserved, even distant, but ask him to share his honey and it will be warm from his smile. ★

PISCES
The Fish
February 20 through March 21

The sign of the Poet or Interpreter
Water Sign
Ruler: Neptune
Gems: Chrysolite, Moonstone, Bloodstone
Color: Sea-Green · Metal: Tin
Compatible Signs: Cancer, Scorpio, Virgo

♥

The Pisces bear is an innocent, susceptible to outside influences. Sensitive, extremely unworldly and impractical, he is always the dreamer, trying to escape from reality. A Pisces bear is often a poet. When you meet a bear who is humble, compassionate, sympathetic and kindly he will probably be born under the sign of the fish. Often they appear bewildered and lost, incapable of running their lives or finding their honey (which they probably gave away). This bear's torrent of emotions is so deep and strong that he may be confused and tormented by it. If ever there is a Teddy Bear saint, he will surely be a Pisces. ★

Monday's bear is fair of face.
Tuesday's bear is full of grace.
Wednesday's bear is full of woe.
Thursday's bear has far to go.
Friday's bear is loving and giving.
Saturday's bear works hard for a living.
But the bear born on the Sabbath day,
Is happy and wise and good and gay.

The Well-Bred TeddyBear

Is it considered polite to hug your Teddy Bear in public? Is it correct to introduce your bear first and then yourself? Should bears be allowed in the dining car of Amtrak trains?

These questions, and others just as compelling, are the domain of one of America's most polite, most proper, most well-bred Teddy Bears, **Ms. Etta-Ketta Bruin**. Known on several continents as the Emily Post of bears, she currently resides in a quiet corner of the den where the afternoon sun filters through the bamboo blinds and gives her fur a golden glow. Ms. Etta-Ketta Bruin has never married but has been the hostess of numerous affairs. She has spread herself around but not too generously as to be considered gauche. And not too thin as to appear cheap!

Looking at her fine mohair coat and pure glass eyes one feels that she was not merely made, but created out of some Victorian fantasy. Truly to the manner born, she lives the quiet, genteel life once reserved for royalty and Southern Belles. Rumor has it that she was a consultant on manners for the film version of *Gone With the Wind*, but that hasn't been confirmed. After all, a proper lady does not boast of accomplishment; she allows others to toot the horn for her.

> *If you hold your nose in the air you are likely to fall flat on your face.*
>
> The World According to HUG

While the following notes on etiquette hardly cover the entire spectrum of possible situations involving bears and their companions, it does present an attitude towards that special relationship between human and

Teddy Bear. To this issue, Ms. Etta-Ketta Bruin speaks most knowledgeably and eloquently. (Was that too loud enough, my dear?)

"Politeness is a virtue, one of the few worth having. It does not hamper one with guilt but the lack of it certainly hampers one's climb up the social scales.

"Never refuse an invitation to an affair that involves either love or honey, as both of these are nourishment for the heart and spirit.

"Correct behavior is entirely based on whether or not it feels good, looks good or tastes good. Remember that good taste is best reserved for the discussion of food.

"I always fly economy with the luxury of two bears.

"Eating in public is delightful if one is not too hungry. The distraction of conversation and passing strangers require one to divert one's attention from the meal.

"Speaking of strangers, never agree to dine with perfect strangers. They are seldom perfect and usually stranger than you'd care for.

It is the charm of bears that they cannot be bored.

The World According to HUG

"As to the question of introductions and what is proper, I have come to this very logical conclusion. Since the humans in question have probably nothing else in common besides their appreciation of Teddy Bears (which is more than quite enough to have in common with anyone) it seems only correct that they introduce their bear first and then themselves. If the situation is that one human is a lady and the other one a gentleman, then the lady person quite naturally has the right of first introduction since human etiquette prevails. This is true in the matter of doors, window seats on planes and whatever else they choose to concern themselves with in the name of chivalry. After all, it was their King Arthur, not ours.

"Should you hug your Teddy Bear in public? Of course you should! Don't you want other people to know you are lovable? Don't you want them to see that you are in the possession of a perfectly delightful Teddy Bear? After all, a little envy is good for the soul. Isn't it?

"Now, it is my feeling that bears and their companion humans should openly cavort together, especially at picnics and by the seashore. I think all winds prevailing, they should sail together, fly together, train together and, while I prefer not to take them myself, bus together.

"The love and affection of man and bear has a long tradition going back to the father of us all, Teddy Roosevelt. If it was good enough for him, it should certainly be good enough for everyone! People without bears to love and be loved by are adrift on the sea of loneliness. Pity them and show them the way. Give them a Teddy Bear.

"And then there is the matter of intimacy. The author of this book was speaking to an assembly of Teddy Bear friends. At the end of his talk he agreed to answer questions from the floor (not always a wise decision, as we will see). After several innocuous questions about

prices and whether or not to remove a Steiff tag, one dear little lady in the front row, her smile too ingenuous to be believed, asked straight out, 'Mr. Menten, do you sleep with your bears?' Of course everyone sleeps with their bears and everyone knows they do, but this sweet thing was out to be cute.

"Ignoring the obvious, Mr. Menten replied, 'Teddy Bears are very private creatures and I certainly do not intend to name names. However, when my beloved human is away, I do sleep with a companion bear.' Now that is what I call taste and tact!"

Well, Ms. Etta-Ketta Bruin, I certainly thank you for the compliment. I'm not sure that one of my many embarrassing public moments is relevant to the discussion of Teddy Bear etiquette, but I am too polite to say so. ♥

HUG

*I enjoy a good talker
but a good hug often
says a whole lot more.*

The World According to HUG

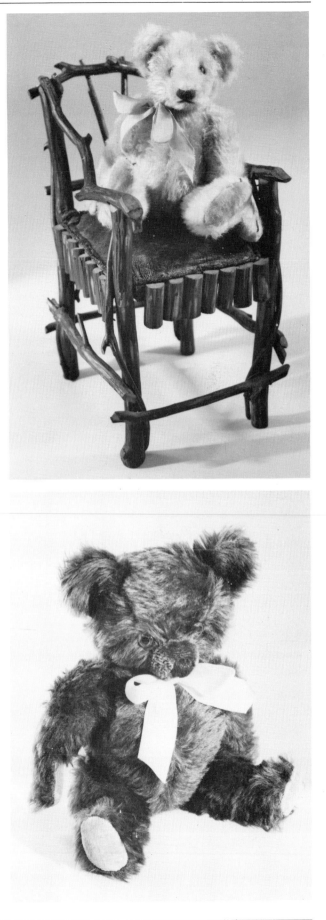

The Gourmet TeddyBear

Put on your aprons and let's enter the magical world of cooking. "Yum, yum and a fat 'round tumtum" sing the bears as they circle the kitchen trying to be helpful and stay out from under foot. OK everyone, this is **Cooking School for Teddy Bears** and their friends, so sit down and take notes.

Rule One: Everything tastes better with honey, if you don't believe me, ask your Teddy.

Rule Two: Don't eat all the honey or you won't be able to cook all these scrumptious goodies.

Rule Three: Always have plenty of honey on hand for special occasions and sudden surprises.

Cooking with honey is easy if you remember a few important things about the nature of honey.

Honey comes in different forms; from right off the comb to straight from the jar. Try all the different types of honey. People have different tastes but bears love them all, no matter what the form.

Here are some helpful hints for cooking with honey. Don't heat honey over 160°, as it could affect the flavor adversely. It is often suggested that honey can be substituted for sugar on a cup-for-cup ratio. This is not always true because honey is usually sweeter than sugar. A good rule when trying this conversion is to reduce the amount by 50%. Better safe than sorry, a too sweet dessert can be a disaster, but a not quite sweet dessert can be called *subtle*.

In puddings, custards and pie fillings it is best to use a 50% ratio. In baking cakes and cookies, ¾ cup for 1 cup will be just about right. If you use honey in a cake recipe instead of sugar, reduce the liquid called for in the recipe by three tablespoons. Honey used in bread, cakes and cookies gives them remarkable keeping qualities as well as a chewy texture and a browner color. Use light colored honey for cooking as dark honey may be disagreeably strong in the recipe.

Now don the Chef's hat, and start cookin'. ♥

Black Forest German Honey Cookies

Here's the perfect cookie to serve with your Steiff Tea Party Bears. Of course, all good bears will love these scrumptdillious crunchies. Thank goodness this recipe makes about two hundred 2½ inch cookies.

- 1 pint honey
- 3 ounces each of citron, candied orange peel and candied lemon peel
- 1 cup chopped blanched almonds
- 1 teaspoon grated lemon rind
- 3 tablespoons cinnamon
- 1 tablespoon cloves
- 3⅓ cups confectioner's sugar
- 6 eggs
- ¼ cup orange juice
- 2 tablespoons hot water
- 5 cups sifted all-purpose flour
- 1 tablespoon baking soda

Cut up into small pieces and combine the citron, orange peel and lemon peel. Add almonds, grated lemon rind, cinnamon, cloves, and confectioner's sugar. Beat mixture until light. Add eggs and orange juice. In a saucepan, combine the honey and water; bring to a boiling point and cool until lukewarm. Stir this mixture into the egg mixture and add flour and baking soda. Mix well. Cover the dough and let stand for 12 hours or longer. Preheat oven to 350°. Drop the batter from a spoon, well apart, on a greased baking sheet. Bake until light brown. Cool.

Queen Bee Honeycomb Pudding

Bees approve this recipe because it requires no honey and so saves them work. A lazy, hibernating bear thought this one up so he wouldn't have to go out looking for a honeycomb.

- 1 cup sugar
- 1 cup flour
- ½ teaspoon baking soda
- 1 cup molasses
- ½ cup butter (melted)
- 1 cup milk
- 4 eggs (well beaten)

Preheat oven to 350°. Butter a 2-quart baking dish. Melt butter and add to warm milk. In large mixing bowl blend sugar, flour and baking soda. Add melted butter and milk mixture. Stir. Add molasses. Beat thoroughly. Stir in 4 well beaten eggs. Stir until mixture is even. Pour into baking dish. Bake 45 minutes or until firm. Serve with Honey-Lemon sauce or Whipped Cream.   *Serves six.*

Honey-Apricot Goo a la Bonkers

This recipe was created by an apricot colored bear who owned a blender and favored bananas. He claimed to have been raised by an orangutan named 'Bonkers'. Well, anything is possible. This goo is great for salads.

- ¼ cup honey
- 1 (8¾-ounce) can unpeeled apricot halves, drained
- 1 cup sour cream
- 1 tablespoon lemon juice
- 1 dash salt

Combine ingredients in blender; blend until smooth. Chill for ½ hour and serve.   *Makes 1¾ cups.*

Wanda June's Honey 'n' Almond Waffles

Wanda June has a sweet tooth, several in fact. Directly after hibernation, she mixes up a batch of these waffles, gobbles them down and takes a nap. That is some kind of recommendation.

- ½ tablespoon honey
- 2½ cups sifted enriched flour
- 4 teaspoons baking powder
- ¾ teaspoon salt
- 1½ tablespoons sugar
- 2 eggs (beaten)
- 2¼ cups milk
- ¾ cup melted shortening or salad oil
- 1 teaspoon almond flavoring

Sift dry ingredients. Combine eggs, milk and shortening. Combine liquid and dry ingredients just before baking; beat smooth. This is a thin batter. Bake in a hot waffle iron. Serve with Honey-Almond Sauce. Makes 10 waffles.

Honey-Almond Sauce

For the bear with a sweet tooth and a plate full of waffles, this is the perfect sauce.

Warm 1 cup liquid honey in a double boiler. Add ¼ cup butter, ¼ teaspoon almond flavoring and a dash of nutmeg. Serve warm over waffles. Makes one cup.

Lemon-Mint Summer Madness

If you are tempted by the clear, clean taste of lemon and the smoothness of a light custard, try this bit of ecstasy. This eye-catching dessert is perfect for a sultry summer night. Caution: Do not serve when the moon is full… it doubles the madness.

- ½ cup honey
- 2 envelopes unflavored gelatin
- 1 cup mint tea
- 4 (8 ounce size) containers plain yogurt
- ½ teaspoon vanilla
- 1 lemon (juice and rind)

In a small saucepan combine honey and unflavored gelatin; stir in mint tea. Let stand five minutes to soften. Heat, stirring often, until gelatin is completely dissolved. Pour into a large bowl and cool. Stir in yogurt, vanilla, lemon juice and rind. With a wire whisk or electric mixer, blend until very smooth. Pour mixture into 1½ quart ring mold and refrigerate overnight. Before serving, dip mold briefly into hot water and gently shake until the custard loosens from the sides of the mold. Place a plate over the top of the mold and invert. Remove mold and garnish with lemon wedges and mint sprigs. To add to the madness, fill the center of the mold with whipped cream.
Serve immediately. *Serves four to six.*

Hug's Milkshake of the Stars

This dreamy recipe will knock your socks off… and it's healthy too. Some people even like to add a couple of raw eggs to this mixture for more protein. If you're a health nut, you might just want to do that.

¼ cup honey
1 cup milk
½ cup plain or vanilla yogurt
1 cup fresh orange juice
¼ cup malted milk powder
¼ cup unsweetened cocoa
1 teaspoon vanilla
1 teaspoon cinnamon

Combine all the ingredients in a blender. Add enough milk to make a full quart. Refrigerate.   *Makes 1 quart.*

Super-Duper Honey Sauce

Thicker and richer sauce for cakes and puddings.

½ cup honey
2 tablespoons melted butter
2 teaspoons cornstarch
1 teaspoon rum or rum flavoring

In a small saucepan mix butter, cornstarch and rum. Stir until smooth. Add honey. Simmer over medium heat for five minutes. Serve at once.

Paddington Station Crunch Cookies

These cookies will take good care of any bear at any time. They can be made with raisins or chocolate chips or nuts or, for that matter, all three together.

½ cup honey
⅓ cup butter (softened)
1 egg
1 teaspoon vanilla
1¼ cups whole-wheat flour
½ teaspoon baking soda
¾ teaspoon salt
1 teaspoon cinnamon
1 cup of raisins, nuts or chocolate chips

Preheat oven to 350°. In a large bowl mix honey and butter with a wooden spoon or egg beater until there are no lumps. Stir in the egg and vanilla. In a separate bowl sift together the flour, baking soda, salt and cinnamon. Pour the flour mixture into the honey-butter mixture and mix until completely blended together. Add raisins or chocolate chips or nuts or any combination that strikes your fancy. Mix everything together and drop teaspoonfuls of dough on an ungreased cookie sheet. Bake 10 to 12 minutes until cookies are golden brown. Let the cookies cool.   *Makes about 50 cookies.*

Strawberry-Honey Whip

Here is a special ice cream treat for young bears and children of all ages. This elegant dessert originated in the Victorian age and is best enjoyed wearing a large straw hat while sitting on a veranda overlooking the sea.

    3 fresh strawberries
    1 cup vanilla ice cream
    ¼ cup honey

Slice the strawberries and arrange them in the bottom of a champagne glass. Blend honey and ice cream in a blender; pour over strawberries and place in freezer for two hours. Top with whipped cream drizzled with honey. Serve at once!   **Serves one.**

Honey-Lemon Sauce

This thin sauce is perfect for cakes and puddings.

    2 tablespoons honey
    ½ cup sugar
    ¼ cup water
    2 teaspoons butter
    1 tablespoon lemon juice

In a small saucepan put honey, sugar and water. Boil 5 minutes without stirring. Remove from heat and add butter and lemon juice. Stir until even. Serve at once.

Uncle Pinch-Penny's Cheap Cake

Uncle Pinch-Penny was a poverty stricken bear who didn't discover the finer things in life until he was very old. This is his favorite recipe because it doesn't use expensive ingredients like eggs or milk or butter. However, rich or poor, this spice cake is a treasure.

    ½ cup honey
    1 cup orange juice
    1 cup shortening
    1 cup raisins and chopped dried apricots
    ½ cup sugar
    1 tablespoon cinnamon
    2 cups whole-wheat flour
    2 teaspoons baking powder
    ½ teaspoon baking soda
    ½ cup sesame seeds or crushed nuts

Preheat oven to 350°. Into a saucepan put honey, orange juice, raisin-apricot mixture, sugar and cinnamon. Boil ingredients for 5 minutes over medium heat. Let mixture cool for an hour or so. Beat until smooth. Sift in flour, baking powder and baking soda. Stir well. Grease an 8-inch loaf pan and pour in batter. Sprinkle top with sesame seeds or nuts. Bake for 45 minutes and let cool in the pan.   **Makes one loaf.**

Rich Man's Honey Frosting

When Uncle Pinch-Penny did finally discover the finer things in life, this frosting was one of them. It will glamorize even his favorite Cheap Cake!

    3 tablespoons honey
    1 teaspoon plain, unsweetened gelatin
    1 tablespoon cold water
    1 cup heavy cream
    1 teaspoon vanilla

Into a small saucepan place the unsweetened gelatin with the tablespoon of cold water. Warm over a medium heat. Stir until all the gelatin is dissolved. Pour cream into a mixing bowl and whip until thick and fluffy. Chill the bowl and the beater for better results. Scrape the gelatin mixture into the whipped cream and add the honey and vanilla. Keep beating until everything is thoroughly blended. Frost the cake. If you don't intend to devour the whole thing right then and there you had better keep it cool.   **Frosts one cake.**

Double Thick Honey-Lemon Sauce

This is a creamy version of Honey-Lemon Sauce. Especially good over gingerbread or spice cake.

    ½ cup honey
    ½ cup heavy cream
    1 teaspoon lemon juice

Beat cream until thick. Beat in honey and lemon juice. Beat until mixture is even. Chill and serve.

Pooh's Banana Pudding in Minutes

Here's a quick delight you can make in minutes for that unexpected visit of hungry bears. Children of all ages like this dessert too.

- 2 tablespoons honey
- 2 tablespoons peanut butter
- ½ cup applesauce
- 2 ripe bananas
- 1 teaspoon cinnamon

Peel bananas and cut into small pieces. Place banana pieces in a large, flat bottom bowl. Mash until smooth. Add honey, applesauce and peanut butter. Stir with a wire whisk until smooth. Chill and serve sprinkled with cinnamon.   *Serves four.*

Orange Sudden Summer Jell

Oh, boy, here's a great treat for hot summer nights. Tasty, tangy and easy to make. And, it looks fantastic with a cherry on top.

- ¼ cup honey
- 1 cup cold water
- 1 package plain gelatin
- 1 small can mandarin oranges
- ½ cup orange juice
- 1 tablespoon lemon juice

In a saucepan put ½ cup water. Sprinkle in gelatin. Cook over a low heat for three minutes; stir constantly until the gelatin is completely dissolved. Remove from stove and stir in honey, ½ cup water, orange and lemon juice. Place orange slices in the bottom of a glass bowl. Pour mixture into bowl and refrigerate until it jells, about two hours. Top with whipped cream.   *Serves six.*

Hibernation Honey Cakes

Many bears hibernate for the winter months. Teddys of course, only hibernate when no one is at home to play with. These cakes are wonderful to come home to after a romp in the snow or a walk in the rain.

- ½ cup honey
- 1 egg
- ¾ cup brown sugar
- ½ cup dark molasses
- 3 cups sifted enriched flour
- 1¼ teaspoons nutmeg
- 1¼ teaspoons cinnamon
- ½ teaspoon cloves
- ½ teaspoon allspice
- ½ teaspoon baking soda
- ½ cup chopped mixed candied fruits and peels
- ½ cup slivered blanched almonds

Preheat oven to 350°. Beat egg, add brown sugar and beat again until fluffy. Stir in the honey and molasses. Sift together dry ingredients and add to first mixture. Mix well until smooth. Stir in fruits, peels and nuts. Chill overnight. Roll ¼ inch thick on floured surface. Cut into rectangles 3½" x 2". Bake on a greased cookie sheet for 12 minutes. Cool before removing.   *Makes 2 dozen.*

Honey and Orange Marmalade 'Muffies'

There are a large number of English Teddys who swear by these muffins and swear even more if they don't get any.

  1 tablespoon honey
  ⅓ cup shortening
  ¼ cup sugar
  2 eggs (well-beaten)
  ½ teaspoon vanilla
  1¾ cups sifted enriched flour
  2 teaspoons baking powder
  ½ teaspoon salt
  ⅓ cup milk
     Orange marmalade

Preheat oven to 375°. Cream shortening and sugar. Add honey, vanilla, and eggs; beat well. Add sifted dry ingredients alternately with milk. Beat the mixture until smooth. Fill greased muffin pans ⅔ full. Drop teaspoon of orange marmalade on the top of each muffin. Bake for twenty minutes. **Makes 12.**

I am at home in my heart and a guest in yours.

The World According to HUG

Boston Tea Party Butter Cake

This butter cake recipe dates back to our forefathers and became a favorite of Teddy Bears living in and around Boston. A large gold Steiff named Wellington served it to me on a brisk autumn day. It is delicious with Honey-Lemon Sauce.

  ½ cup honey
  1¾ cups pastry or cake flour
  ½ teaspoon salt
  2 teaspoons baking powder
  ⅓ cup butter
  ½ teaspoon vanilla
  2 eggs (separate whites and yolks)
  ½ cup milk
  ½ teaspoon ginger
  ½ teaspoon cinnamon

Preheat oven to 350°. Butter a 9" x 9" x 2" pan. Sift together the cake flour, salt, baking powder, ginger and cinnamon. In a separate bowl, cream the butter thoroughly, add vanilla and gradually beat in honey. Beat until fluffy. Beat in 2 egg yolks. Stir in ½ cup of the flour mixture. Stir in ¼ cup milk. Mix. Add the rest of the flour mixture and beat just enough to blend well. Beat 2 egg whites until they stand up in soft peaks; fold into batter. Spoon into pan. Bake 30 minutes. Note: When using an electric mixer, do not separate the eggs. Add the creamed butter and honey one at a time, beating well. **Makes one cake.**

Sticky Fingers Sauce

This gooey delight is a perfect topping for ice cream or pudding and it makes a great sauce to dip fresh fruit into. It will even make your fingers taste better!

- ½ cup honey
- ¼ cup hot water
- ¼ cup chopped nut meats
- ¼ cup minced candied orange or lemon peel
- ½ teaspoon ginger or cinnamon

Combine ingredients in a small saucepan and stir well over a low heat. Chill and serve.   *Makes one cup.*

Honey Bear's Southern Comfort Sauce

Miss Scarlet O'Beara served this sauce over fresh fruit and became the toast of Atlanta. Socially speaking, it pays to have a Honey Bear for a friend.

- 2 tablespoons honey
- ½ cup fresh orange juice
- 2 tablespoons lemon juice
- ⅛ cup finely chopped fresh mint

Combine until completely blended. Serve chilled over fresh fruit, garnish with mint leaves.   *Makes ¾ cup.*

Tree-top Honey-Bee Glaze

This glaze is perfect for breakfast cakes and will cover two 9-inch squares.

- ¼ cup honey
- ½ cup sugar
- ¼ cup milk
- ¼ cup butter
- ½ cup crushed nut meats

Combine ingredients in a sauce pan. Stir and bring to the boiling point over low heat. Spread over coffee cakes that are ready to be baked.   *Makes ¾ cup.*

Roman Delight Sesame Honey Clusters

Caesar Bear, the last Roman Emperor Bear, savored these clusters as he marched about conquering bee-hives by the score. They are healthy and hearty and will stick to your ribs with goodness. Otherwise there would be no reason to eat them.

- ¼ cup honey
- ¼ cup butter
- ½ cup sesame seeds
- 1 cup grated coconut
- ½ teaspoon vanilla
- ½ cup crushed almonds

Melt butter in a large frying pan over a low heat. Stir in sesame seeds and coconut. Stir mixture around for five minutes over low heat. Remove pan from stove and add vanilla and honey. After the honey is all mixed in, put the candy in a cold place until it gets stiff enough to shape into balls. About an hour in the refrigerator should be long enough. Roll the candy into little balls and press one end into the crushed almonds. Serve and enjoy. Keep the ones you don't eat in the refrigerator.   *Makes 3 dozen.*

A clown is more courageous
than a lion tamer,
he dares to amuse.

The World According to HUG

Applause is not necessary.
A simple thank you
will do.

The World According to HUG

Teddy Goes to the Movies

Quiet! Quiet on the set! Lights…Camera…Action! This is a movie and this is Hollywood, land of make-believe and enchantment. What better place for a talented Teddy Bear? After all, who knows more about enchantment and make-believe than Teddy, the master of disguise and the spinner of dream webs? Here, in this sunny world of fast cars and movie stars, the Teddy Bear is naturally a success. Or is he?

True, the coveted role of Scarlett went to Vivien and of course Clark got the Rhett part. Then there was that deadly ego blow dealt by the choice of humans to play the parts of the Munchkins in the Oz epic.

True, the Star Wars saga more than made up for that with the Teddy Bear inspired Ewoks but real stardom has craftily eluded the Teddy Bear.

Of course there was a bear in *Rich and Famous* but he ended up being torn in half by two screaming women in a raging argument. Not a pretty sight.

Then in *Compulsion*, Teddy represented the darker side of one of the killers and was quite convincing. At least he wasn't typecast. He appeared in *John and Mary* with Dustin and Mia and in several others like *Die, Die My Darling* with Tallulah Bankhead. Sal Mineo was in a flick called *Who Killed Teddy Bear?* And the beautiful Ava Gardner once played a character named Honey Bear (*Mogambo*).

> ## Success is the result of a headlong plunge, not a furtive step.
>
> *The World According to HUG*

And, while Teddy made it to Broadway in *The Curious Savage* with Lillian Gish and *Strange Interlude*

In his wonderful book called *The Teddy Bear Book,* Peter Bull tells the story of *Delicatessen's* rise from a poor working class bear (he was originally employed by a Dry Goods Store) to international stardom.

In 1983, *Paddington* starred in his own special on Cable TV and it is hoped that more roles will be available for talented bears in the future. And have you noticed how many bears are appearing in TV commercials? They know where the money is, and the first step to Hollywood. ♥

with Geraldine Page, it took television to bring Teddy into clear focal stardom.

First there was the wonderful relationship between *Radar* and his Teddy Bear in many of the *M.A.S.H.* plots. Then came Teddy's shining hour, *Brideshead Revisited.* The leading part of the Teddy Bear was awarded to a bear named *Delicatessen* who is the faithful friend of Peter Bull. In the production, the character is called *Aloysius* and he is the companion bear to the character, *Lord Sebastian Flyte* played by Anthony Andrews.

HUG

The Musical TeddyBear

The year was 1957, and Elvis Presley was America's heartthrob. Paramount Pictures released his film, *Loving You* and later that year the title song came out as a single with "(Let Me Be Your)Teddy Bear" on the flip side. The song was written by Karl Mann and Bernie Lowe and was tailor-made for Elvis' passion for Teddy Bears. Within a few months, Elvis was pelvis-deep in cuddly, lovable bears. Elvis recorded this song on several albums including the 1957 LP *Loving You, Vol. 1*. Later, it appeared on the LP's; *Elvis Golden Records, Elvis: Worldwide Gold Award Hits, Volume 1, Elvis As Recorded At Madison Square Garden,* and several others, including *Elvis Sings For Children (And Grown-Ups Too)* which was released in 1978.

While this was hardly Elvis' greatest hit, it sure was popular with the Teddy Bears and their friends.

Another great favorite with Teddy Bears is the song *The Teddy Bears Picnic* by John W. Bratton. This favorite

has been beautifully presented by Green Tiger Press as a book and record combination. The charming illustrations show the bears at play and enjoying the famous picnic.

> *A braggart is*
> *a small bear*
> *with a big drum.*
>
> The World *According to HUG*

Teddy Bear songs have ranged from rags to marches, including *The Little Teddy Bears Dress Ball, The Teddy Bear March, Teddy Bear's Lullaby* and one number called *Stung* by Theron C. Bennett which involves a bee and a bear, not an unlikely event.

During the first rush of their popularity in the early

1900s, Teddy Bears were the subject of many songs and ballads, most of which have unfortunately been put on the musical back shelf.

Another musical version of the Teddy Bear mania was the Teddy Bear with a music box inside. Recently this sort of bear has been revived by bear makers and one of my favorites is a bear called Autry who plays *Don't Fence Me In.*

There are a great number of music box bears sitting atop musical devices as well as those with tunes in their tummies.

You are your own best clown.

The World According to HUG

And finally, there are those clever fellows who play musical instruments when you wind them up. These bears usually are attired in band uniforms and make a great racket beating a drum and blowing a whistle. They are often cute, and just as often a calamity! I suppose it is a matter of which you prefer—music or bears. ♥

TeddyBear Dot-to-Dot
Connect the dots and color the picture.
(Solution on page 159)

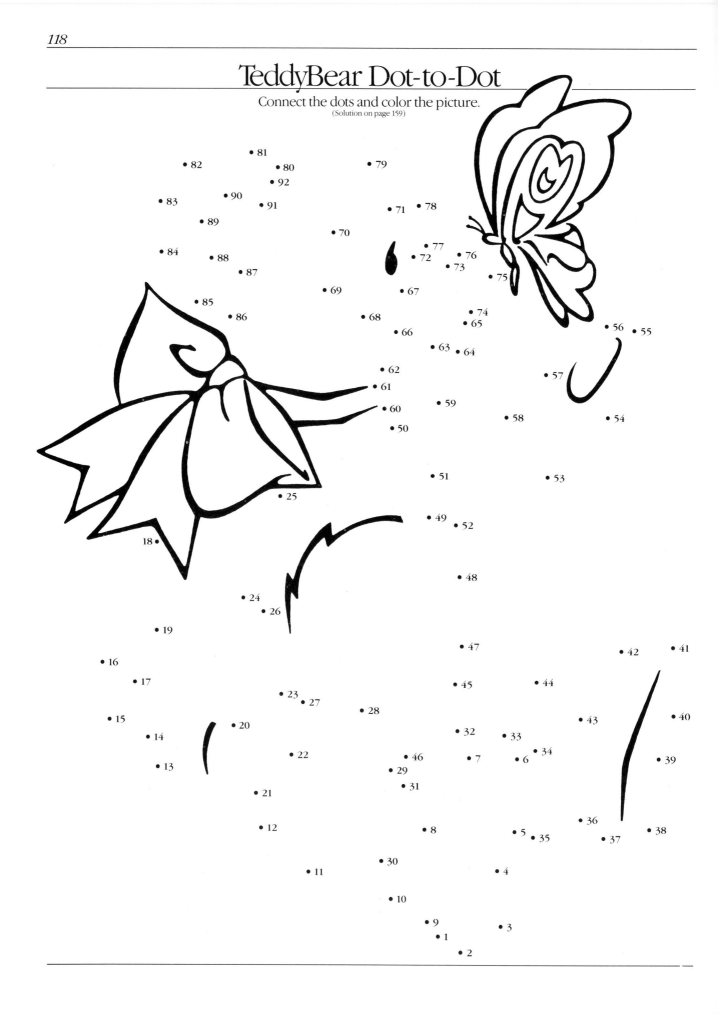

TeddyBear Puzzles

(Solutions on page 159)

This Teddy Bear has made four lines on his tablet. Can you add five more lines and make TEN?

This Teddy Bear casts a shadow. Find the correct silhouette that matches the drawing.

Which of these bears is the tallest? Hint: This is an optical illusion.

TeddyBear Clubs & Publications

Many Teddy Bear fans join together and form a club. These groups usually meet on a more or less regular basis and have fun and exchange stories about their bears. Generally speaking, a Teddy Bear Club is dedicated to the enjoyment of bears and their human companions and any relevant information exchanged is strictly an added bonus to the fun and games.

There are Teddy Bear Conventions or Rallies in many cities around the country. The Philadelphia zoo has had an event or two and in New York City, people gather at the posh Algonquin Hotel and celebrate Pooh's birthday.

Organized or not, Teddy's friends love to gather and enjoy themselves. Another way of getting together is the newsletter or publication.

In 1983, Hobby House Press introduced a magazine for Teddys called *The Teddy Bear and friends.* And I have my own club and newsletter called *International Bearhugs.*

> *By the time a man's opinion has any value, he may have overspent it.*
>
> The World According to HUG

But, the very best Teddy Bear publication in the whole wide world is *The Teddy Tribune.*

Founded in 1980 by Barbara Wolters and edited by a charming bear named Dumper, *The Teddy Tribune* is the very backbone of the bear world. There are many other newsletters and club bulletins as well as mailers from stores that specialize in Teddy Bears, but they are not as comprehensive.

The Teddy Tribune is a big, thick bundle of wonder, filled with pictures and stories as well as ads for new bears and bear related items. Dumper has his own Bears Only Club that has had a running feud going on between himself and some dissident rabbits who insist that they have a right to join the club. The letters that are exchanged between these two factions are worth a hundred laughs and the price of admission.

While there are slicker publications, none can match the wit and enthusiasm that Barbara and Dumper bring to the world of Teddy Bears. They have perfect rapport…perfect harmony…perfect karma.

So, if you love your Teddy Bear, get yourself and him a subscription to The Teddy Tribune. Do it now!   ♥

The Teddy Tribune
254 W. Sidney St.
St. Paul, MN 55107

Bearhugs
300 E. 40th St., Box 28K
New York, NY 10016

HUG's World
300 E. 40th St., 28K
New York, NY 10016

**The Teddy Bear
and friends magazine**
900 Frederick St.
Cumberland, MD 21502

Teddy Bears Lovers Club
c/o The Enchanted Valley Doll
Hospital and Bear Refuge
1412 Carver Rd.
Modesto, CA 95350

**Good Bears
of the World International**
P.O. Box 8236
Honolulu, HI 96815

Bears Only Club
254 W. Sideny St.
St. Paul, MN 55107

International Bearhugs
300 E. 40th St., Box 28K
New York, NY 10016

The HUG Club
300 E. 40th St., Box 28K
New York, NY 10016

The Literary TeddyBear

The Teddy Bear has certainly captured the imagination of storytellers and writers since his debut in 1903. From *Paddington* to *Pooh, Rupert* to *Aloysius,* these guys have made a name for themselves in print.

Likewise, their counterpart/inspiration/alter ego, the natural bear, has also been immortalized in hundreds of stories from *Snow White and Rose Red* to the tale of *Goldilocks and the Three Bears,* perhaps the most famous of all bear tales.

American Indian legends tell many stories of bears as do ancient Greek myths. And in all this literature one theme seems to prevail, the bear is good. No other animal or animal character in fiction enjoys the constant depiction of love and benevolence that the Teddy Bear and the natural bear do.

While a few bears are occasionally naughty or pull off a prank or two, they are never really bad. Throughout all literature, legend, and myth, the bear is seen as a symbol of gentleness and love. There is a bit of irony here because in reality the bear is a dangerous and formidable adversary in his natural habitat. While the gentle Teddy Bear and the slow moving bears of the circus and zoo charm and delight us, we shouldn't forget his wild counterpart in the forest.

> *When Pinocchio told a lie,*
> *his nose got bigger.*
> *If a Teddy Bear told a lie,*
> *his heart would get smaller.*
>
> *The World According to HUG*

Perhaps the Teddy Bear, beginning life as he did, inspired by an act of kindness, has captured our hearts and imaginations. And we need him to convey this spirit of loving and caring to the world around us. ♥

If you would know a Teddy
...search your own heart.

The World According to HUG

The TeddyBear Catalog
by Peggy & Alan Bialosky
Published by:
Workman Publishing Company, Inc.
1 W. 39th St.
New York, NY 10018

A Collector's History of the Teddy Bear
by Patricia N. Schoonmaker
Published by:
Hobby House Press, Inc.
900 Frederick St.
Cumberland, MD 21502

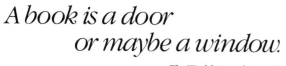

*A book is a door
or maybe a window.*

The World According to HUG

The Teddy Book
by Peter Bull
Published by:
House of Nisbet Ltd.
Winscombe, England

The World According to HUG
by Ted Menten
Published by:
Delilah Communications
118 E. 25th St.
New York, NY 10010

*Being misquoted isn't so bad
...it shows that someone
was almost listening.*

The World According to HUG

Teddy Bears and How To Make Them
by Margaret Hutchings
Published by:
Dover Publications, Inc.
180 Varick St.
New York, NY 10014

My Circle of Bears
by Michele Durkson Clise
Published by:
The Green Tiger Press
La Jolla, CA 92038

Listening well is a virtue.
Speaking well, an art.

The World According to HUG

Stamp It, Teddy. Stamp It!

Oh, they joy of stamping! Be it with colorful stickers that abound in the marketplace today or with rubber stamps that create endless varieties of images by themselves or in combination with other stamps. A good rubber stamp design will have a sense of rhythm or movement that lets you storytell. Many rubber stamps are too static and, after one or two impressions, leave a bit to be desired, so keep that in mind when you buy a rubber stamp. But even the dullest stamp can be fun when colored or repeated in a border. If you make a mistake, make the most of it.

There are lots of wonderful rubber stamps available to choose from, especially through mail-order catalogs. Usually Teddy Bear stores carry an assortment of stamps as well as ink pads and markers for coloring.

Here are some rubber stamping ideas that were suggested to me by one of my favorite companies, *Inkadinkado* in Boston.

To get the effect of a multicolored image, color the stamp directly with water-based colored markers. Stamp a piece of paper and you'll see that all the colors you put on the stamp have been transferred to the paper.

> *A poet is a realist
> with a flower
> behind his ear.*
>
> The World According to HUG

For another colorful effect, stamp your design in black ink, wait until it is completely dry, then color in the areas with watercolors or markers.

If you want to get really fancy, stamp a row of bears to form a chorus line. Or, try blanking out part of your design with a piece of paper so that when you stamp you get just a part of the image. Then you can add on part of another image or draw in another design yourself to complete the picture.

Rubber stamps work well in conjunction with stickers or just by themselves. However you use them, they are lots of fun and are a personal, decorative touch to all your Teddy Bear correspondence.

One Teddy Bear lover has put together a whole catalog of Teddy Bear rubber stamps from the various companies that manufacture them.

There are over 400 designs in the catalog and you can get more information about the catalog and stamps, by writing to: **T. Bearstamps**, 7722 South Butte Avenue, Tempe, AZ 85284. Enclose an SASE with your request. ♥

INKADINKADO, Inc.
102 South St.
Boston, MA 02111

All Night Media
Box 227
Forest Knolls, Ca 94933

Bizzaro Rubber Stamp Catalogue
P.O. Box 126, Annex Station
Providence, RI 02901

Hero Arts
P.O. Box 5234
Berkeley, CA 94703

Readance Rubber Stamp Service
10617 Linnet Ave.
Cleveland, OH 44111

17th Street Rubber Works
110 E. 17th St., Apt. 2F
New York, NY 10003

The Rubber Stamp Catalog
P.O. Box 209
Bristol, RI 02809

Rubberstampede
1572 Euclid Ave.
Berkeley, CA 94708

Grays Harbor Stamp Works
110 N. G St.
Aberdeen, WA 98520

The Bear Tender
5935 Lyndale Ave. N.
Brooklyn Center, MN 55430

Rubber Stamp Fun

Have some fun. Color in the stamp designs
and write captions inside the speech ballons.

The Honey Heist Maze

Here is a double maze. There are two ways that you can play.
1) Enter at the bottom, pick up the honey and exit at the top.
2) Or two bears play, each enters at the same time, one at the top and the other at the bottom.
Race to see who gets to the honey first. Have fun!

(Solution on page 159)

How to Make a TeddyBear Jumping Jack

Mount the drawing on heavy paper and cut out. Punch out holes marked ⊗ Use ½″ brass paper fasteners to assemble figure as shown. Fasten loosely so figure will move easily. Use large needle with heavy thread to string figure. Single black dot indicates where to string arms and legs. Tie string straight across when arms and legs are straight down. Then tie control string to center of arm and leg strings. Now hold head and pull control string down. When you pull down on control string the arms and legs should move upward. When you let go of the control string, arms and legs should fall back easily.

The Making of a TeddyBear

While not every Teddy Bear aficionado has the talent, time or energy to create a bear of their very own, most dream of that special bear they might create, given the talent, time and energy.

There are many wonderful patterns and kits available for the novice bearmaker and they are a good starting point if the idea of drafting an original pattern turns your fingers into five thumbs. Relax, this is really a lot of fun.

Start with a simple, nonjointed Teddy Bear pattern. After you have mastered that pattern, revise it on your own to make it taller or fatter or have a longer nose. Try several variations on that original pattern. Once you understand how the pattern works, create one completely on your own. This is basic on-the-job-training for bear makers. Then try the same procedure for a jointed Teddy Bear.

Experiment with fabrics. Use inexpensive plush or velvet or terrycloth or felt for your first bears. Don't start with mohair as it is too costly to use on these trial runs. Wait until you have reached a state-of-the-art perfection and then indulge yourself with a yard or two of imported mohair.

If you would be generous, learn it first at the hand of others.

The World According to HUG

The whole idea of making a Teddy Bear of your own design is to experience the joy of creation and the wonder of the phrase—*I did it myself!* So, have fun, make a Teddy! ♥

TeddyBear Crafts

There are many ways to craft a Teddy. You can sew one on the sewing machine or by hand. You can knit or crochet one. Carve one out of wood or cast one in bisque. You can quilt him, stencil him, embroider him or even make him out of stained glass.

There are many wonderful Teddy Bear kits as well as other craft related items that have Teddy for a theme.

One of the most interesting sources for Teddy Bear crafts and repair items is *The Crafty Teddy.* Created by Steve Gardner (who incidently runs *Doll and Craft World* and has the greatest sources you can imagine), this emporium of bear supplies will send you into a tailspin of delight.

Here in one catalog are all the items you will need to create Teddy Bears and Teddy Bear related crafts. There are kits and patterns for bears; patterns for clothes as well as fantastic couture fashions for the bear …ready-made. Beautiful embroidered and smocked

fashions for milady and sweaters and rompers for him!

There are hats and flowers and ribbons and jewelry and umbrella forms and more. So much more!

The kiss of death is the word almost.

The World According to HUG

Beside the craft items, *The Crafty Teddy* has a fine line of plush and imported mohair as well as stuffing and joints…even old-fashioned glass eyes for bears!

So whether you want to make a bear or simply dress one up, this is the place for you! ♥

The Crafty Teddy
125 Eighth St.
Brooklyn, NY 11215

*No one will say
you have a swell head
if you wear
an oversized hat.*

The World According to HUG

HUG

WITH HEARTS, IT'S NOT THE SIZE BUT THE QUALITY.

Here is a design that you can color or use as an embroidery design.

Here is a design that you can color or use as a stained glass pattern.

Here is a design that you can color or use as a stained glass pattern.

Here is a design that you can color or use as an applique pattern.

Here is a design that you can color or use as an applique pattern.

Here is a design that you can color or use as an embroidery design.

Here is a design that you can color or use as an embroidery design.

Here is a design that you can color or use as a stained glass pattern.

Here is a design that you can color or use as an applique pattern.

Here is a design that you can color or use as an embroidery design.

Here is a design that you can color or use as an applique pattern.

Here is a design that you can color or use as a stained glass pattern.

Ein Tier von Steiff. Für immer Dein.

In Search of Golden Bears

So now you want a Teddy Bear of your very own or you want to find the perfect bear for a special friend or someone you love. But now you are wondering where to find that perfect bear. There are several ways to find a Teddy Bear. You can go to your local Toy Store or Department Store and browse over their assortment. Usually these stores, like Macy's or the famous F.A.O. Schwarz toy store, have a good selection of modern, commercially made Teddy Bears. They will usually carry all or part of the Steiff line of quality bears and other animals as well as Gund or Hermann, another fine German line of Teddy Bears.

Many gift shops and greeting card stores carry stuffed toys and Teddy Bears as well as Teddy Bear inspired items like the wonderful *Lucy and Me* figurines and cards designed by Lucy Rigg.

If you are looking for an older, experienced bear you might try antique shops, where you are likely to find a wonderful old bear at an equally wonderful price. The local Goodwill stores often have delightful bears at delightful prices and you might find a real winner while helping a good cause. The Church Bazaar, Street Fair or Block Party often have bears and even some handmade ones created by local artists and talented grandmothers.

TeddyBear:
*   price on the ticket;*
*   value in the heart.*

The World According to HUG

So-called Flea Markets which once held bargains and now seem overflowing with knockoff designer jeans and very plastic trinkets, are not the joy they once were.

There are, however, some good ones around the country and those lucky enough to be in their area report sightings of splendid bears.

Now if you are an inveterate shopper and a compulsive consumer as I am, then you will seek out and find all manner of Teddy Bears, for they are everywhere.

But there is no better place to shop for bears than a store entirely devoted to Teddy Bears. Imagine it, a whole store filled exclusively with bears!

The windows filled with bears, the shelves overflowing with bears six deep, and everywhere there are bears sitting around smiling or taking afternoon tea laced with honey.

A wonderland of bears, just filled to the rafters with those charming, loving, huggable, irresistible bundles of joy. Whoopee!

Bears filled with soft down or recycled bank notes and made of imported mohair or soft plush, velvet or felt. Bears dressed up in hats and scarfs or in T-shirts, sweaters or tuxedo jackets. Bears six feet tall or so tiny they are no bigger than your thumb. Bears, bears and more bears.

Welcome to the Teddy Bear store! This is it, folks, if you love Teddy Bears and you can't ever, ever get enough of them. If you are contemplating building a new wing onto your house just to give them a playroom or selling your car so that you can convert the garage into a Teddy Bear haven, then this is your kind of store.

The first time I walked into *The Ready Teddy*, I thought I'd died and gone to Teddy Bear lover's heaven!

The Ready Teddy is in San Francisco. Actually, there are two of them a few blocks apart, and they are the brainchild of Nancy Olsen. Nancy runs the business and manages the store at Pier 39, while the other store is presided over by her mother. Imagine how much fun it must be to sit around in a store full of Teddys all day with nothing to do but watch people get happy buying a Teddy Bear. Looks good to me but I'll wager it's hard work, and think of all the honey those bears eat!

The Ready Teddy is just one of several fabulous stores devoted exclusively to Teddy Bears. Just across the bridge from San Francisco in Berkeley is another terrific shop named *Bears to Go*. The afternoon I visited them I made quite a spectacle of myself as I loaded up on furry critters.

In New York City there is the new *Teddy's* in Soho; it's small but it's wonderful.

Most of these stores also have a catalog and do a mail-order business. Both *The Ready Teddy* and *Bears to Go* have newsletters that present new items and discuss special events of interest to the Teddy Bear fan.

Many of the stores listed here are devoted exclusively to retailing Teddy Bears and related items, while others may carry other items as well, like dolls or other stuffed critters.

If you are traveling around America you might want to visit some of these shops along the way. The serious collector as well as the just beginning one will certainly find a warm reception and a friendly hello at these

stores, for it is my experience that Teddy Bear people are as huggable as their furry friends.

It is a good idea to write or phone ahead if you can. I just missed meeting Joan Venturino, who runs *Bears to Go*, because I just dropped by without checking ahead to see if she would be there. And remember that if you are writing to a store it is polite to include an SASE with your letter.

OK gang, saddle up and get your hunting gear ready, this is where the Teddy Bear hunt begins. ♥

ALABAMA

Betsy's on Ross
106 N. Ross St.
Auburn, AL 36830

ARIZONA

Circus
501 S. Mill Ave.
Tempe, AZ 85281

Pretty Pets & Bear Friends
1060 E. Baseline Rd.
Tempe, AZ 85283

CALIFORNIA

The Bear Tree
1240 S. Beach Blvd.
Anaheim, CA 92804

Bears To Go
1400 Shattuck Ave.   #4
Berkeley, CA 94709

Bear Street
415 W. Foothill Blvd.
Claremont, CA 91711

Bear Essentials
1290 Detroit Ave.
Concord, CA 94520

The Bear Fax
122 E. Prospect Ave.
Danville, CA 94526

Discoveries
213 E St.
Davis, CA 95616

Critters
17200 Ventura Blvd.
Encino, CA 91316

Jeanie's Place
10214 Fair Oaks Blvd.
Fair Oaks, CA 95628

Hibernation Station
16574 Walnut
Fountain Valley, CA 92708

Elliott's
11751 Westminster Ave.
Garden Grove, CA 92643

The Friendly Beasts
1141 Prospect St.
La Jolla, CA 92037

The Bear Hug
179 Lakewood Center Mall
Lakewood, CA 90714

Earth Bound
6314B E. Pacific Coast Hwy.
Long Beach, CA 90803

The Wee Leprachaun
6316D E. Pacific Coast Hwy.
Long Beach, CA 90803

Porto Bello
21 Princess St.
Sausalito, CA 94965

Bear With Us
1532 S. Bentley Ave.
Los Angeles, CA 90025

Bears In The Wood
59 N. Santa Cruz Ave.
Los Gatos, CA 95030

Bear to Bear
21217 Pacific Coast Hwy.
Malibu, CA 90265

Bear Comforts
809 Santa Cruz Ave.
Menlo Park, CA 94025

Pilgrim
108 E. Colorado Blvd.
Monrovia, CA 91016

Tex's Toys
655 S. San Antonio Rd.
Mountain View, CA 94040

Nana's Teddies
908 Main St.
Napa, CA 94558

A Little Something Special
5681 Freeport Blvd.
Sacramento, CA 95822

Susan's Store Room
239 San Anselmo Ave.
San Anselmo, CA 94960

Hug A Bear
849 W. Harbor Dr., Suite A
San Diego, CA 92101

The Ready Teddy
Pier 39
San Francisco, CA 94133

Tempty Bears and Toys
15 Fleming Ave.
San Jose, CA 95127

Objects of my Affections
186 Mission Valejo Mall
Mission Valejo, CA 92691

**Enchanted Valley Doll
Hospital & Bear Refuge**
1700 McHenry Village Way
Modesto, CA 95350

Bear-Wee-Wuvables
4463 Meadowlark Dr.
Napa, CA 94558

Campbell's Corner
36534 Ruschin Dr.
Newark, CA 94560

**Dollsville Showroom
& Bearsville Bears**
373 S. Palm Canyon Dr.
Palm Springs, CA 92262

Hug A Bear
245 S. Palm Canyon Dr.
Palm Springs, CA 92262

Two Shoe Bear Co.
2667 N. Palm Canyon Dr.
Palm Springs, CA 92262

Thom's Toys & Things
148 Fleming Ave.
San Jose, CA 95127

Teddy Bear's Picnic
1203 Lincoln Ave.
San Jose, CA 95125

Fuzzy Wuzzy
233 Hillsdale Mall
San Mateo, CA 94403

Just Bearly Enterprises
1606 Stonewood Ct.
San Pedro, CA 90732

Paws & Petticoats
15742½ Groveoak Dr.
Santa Ana, CA 92680

Beary Wonderful
1325 Pacific Ave.
Santa Cruz, CA 95060

Bear Facts
2420 Sonoma Ave.
Santa Rosa, CA 95402

Bizaar Imports
535 Santa Rosa Plaza
Santa Rosa, CA 94501

Teddy Bear's Picnic
122 Oak Ln.
Scott's Valley, CA 95066

Fox Run
720 Holbrook
Simi Valley, CA 93065

Bear 'n Grin It
261 Del Amo Fashion Ctr.
Torrance, CA 90503

The Toy Cellar
6526 Washington St.
Yountville, CA 94599

Bearies & Cream
12124 Saratoga-
Sunnyvale Rd.
Saratoga, CA 95070

**Lions and Tigers
and Bears…oh my!**
110 S. Hope Ave.   #51-D
Santa Barbara, CA 93105

**Bea's House of
Dolls & Teddies**
9438 Magnolia Ave.
Riverside, CA 92503

COLORADO

Bear Hugs Inc.
1421 Larimer Sq.
Denver, CO 80202

Completely Bear Ltd.
300 Fillmore St.
Denver, CO 80206

CONNECTICUT

Particularly Bears
Center Rd.
Easton, CT 06612

Wildflower
57 Maple St.
Ellington, CT 06029

The Fantasy Den
25 Morehouse Ave.
Stratford, CT 06497

Good Hearted Bears
3 Pearl St.
Mystic, CT 06355

DELAWARE

Mr. Bear, Inc.
2642 Capitol Dr.
Newark, DE 19711

DISTRICT OF COLUMBIA

Turtle Park Toys
4733 Fulton St. NW
Washington, DC 20007

FLORIDA

Great Gifts! Inc.
830 NE 27th Ave.
Hallandale, FL 33009

Toys Ahoy!
28 Perwinkle Pl.
Sanibel Island, FL 33957

Sally Fine Classics
1668 Main St.
Sarasota, FL 33577

ILLINOIS

Just Bears
403 Kingsbury
Arlington Heights, IL 60004

Non Pariel
23000 N. Clark
Chicago, IL 60614

Saturday's Child
2146 Halsted St.
Chicago, IL 60614

Beauty and the Beast
835 N. Michigan Ave.
Chicago, IL 60611

Balloons to You
961 W. Webster
Chicago, IL 60614

Gigi's & Sherry's
7900 N. Milwaukee
Niles, IL 60648

Bear Country
108½ E. Main St.
Olney, IL 62450

JBJ
1717 Philo Rd.
Urbana, IL 61801

INDIANA

Bird & Acorn
202 E. Third
Bloomington, IN 47401

IOWA

Winnie's Toy Orphanage
2401 Harding Rd.
Des Moines, IA 50310

KANSAS

Serendipity
111 W. Chestnut
Garden City, KS 67846

Taylor's Toys
1025 Main St.
Great Bend, KS 67530

The Toy Store
709 Kansas Ave.
Topeka, KS 66603

Toys by Roy
7700 E. Kellogg St.
Wichita, KS 67207

MARYLAND

The Calico Teddy
22 E. 24th St.
Baltimore, MD 21218

Grrreat Bears, Ltd.
301 S. Light St.
Baltimore, MD 21202

Toys & Treasures
513 Liberty St.
Hagerstown, MD 21740

Under the Lilac
10101 Balsamwood Dr.
Laurel, MD 20708

Dallas Alice
1047 Taft St.
Rockville, MD 20850

Grin 'N Bear It
9113 Fifth St.
Seabrook, MD 20706

MASSACHUSETTS

Bears Wares
60 Great Rd.
Acton, MA 01720

Bear Packets
22 Hamilton Rd.
Arlington, MA 01274

Geppetto's Toys
Faneuil Hall Marketplace
Boston, MA 02109

Bearly In Business
3811 Main St.
Brewster, MA 02631

Bear-in-Mind
73 Indian Pipe Ln.
Concord, MA 02109

The Gracious Goose
46 Inn St.
Newburyport, MA 01950

Driftwood Cottage
91 Main St.
Rockwood, MA 01966

Bear Hugs, Inc.
41 Oakridge Rd.
Wellesley, MA 02181

MICHIGAN

Stuffed Safari
31065 Orchard Lake Rd.
Farmington Hills, MI 48018

Teddy & Me
202 S. Bridge St.
Grand Ledge, MI 48837

Toy Village
3105 W. Saginaw
Lansing, MI 48917

The Children's Shop
2672 N. Eastman Rd.
Midland, MI 48640

The Carousel
111 Kent St.
Portland, MI 48875

MINNESOTA

The Afton Toy Shop
32900 St. Croix Tr. S.
Afton, MN 55001

Hobbitat, Inc.
110 Westbrook Mall
Brooklyn Ctr., MN 55480

Toyworks
3515 W. 69th St.
Edina, MN 55435

The Teddy Bear Shop
455 Amber Lake Dr.
Fairmont, MN 56031

**Gambucci/
Our Own Hardware**
1312 E. 13th Ave.
Hibbing, MN 55746

Reindeer House
2409 W. 44th St.
Minneapolis, MN 55410

Toyworks
100 N. Sixth St.
Minneapolis, MN 55410

The Tuffet Express
1316 Fourth St. SE
Minneapolis, MN 55414

Toy World
13021 Ridgedale Dr.
Minnetonka, MN 55343

Basquin's Antiques
3060 S. Owasso Blvd.
Roseville, MN 55113

Briar Patch
867 Grand Ave.
St. Paul, MN 55105

MISSISSIPPI

Sherry's
318 Harding St.
Hattiesburg, MS 39401

MISSOURI

Cheri's Bear Essentials
3953 Broadway
Kansas City, MO 64111

Finders Keepers
Main and Mill Sts.
Parkville, MO 64152

Bear Hollow
240 Linden
St. Louis, MO 63105

NEW JERSEY

Diane's Precious Pony
602 Route 71
Brielle, NJ 08730

Meyer's Toy Store
595 Route 18
East Brunswick, NJ 08816

Bea Skydell's
476 Union Ave.
Middlesex, NJ 08846

Beautiful Things Factory
1838 E. Second St.
Scotch Plains, NJ 07076

NEW MEXICO

Tidbits
105 E. Marcy St.
Santa Fe, NM 87801

NEW YORK

Best of Everything
8204 Third Ave.
Brooklyn, NY 11209

The Cooper Shop
Red Mill, Route 23
Claverack, NY 12513

The Rainbow's End
11 Parrott St.
Cold Spring, NY 10516

Bears Etc.
93 Main St.
Cold Spring Harbour,
NY 11724

Delightful Dolls & Toys
307 Cyprus Ln.
Endicott, NY 12760

Littlethings
113 Main St.
Irvington, NY 10533

Treasure Trove
19 Village Rd.
Manhasset, NY 11030

Little Darlings
892 Jericho Tpke.
Nesconset, NY 11767

The Enchanted Forest
85 Mercer St.
New York, NY 10012

The Weill Gallery
68 Thompson St.
New York, NY 10012

Sweet Nellie
1262 Madison Ave.
New York, NY 10028

Le Bear Boutique
506 Amsterdam Ave.
New York, NY 10024

Go Fly A Kite
1201 Lexington Ave.
New York, NY 10028

Geppetto's
South Street Seaport
New York, NY 10038

The Gingerbread House
9 Christopher St.
New York, NY 10003

Dollsandreams
1421 Lexington Ave.
New York, NY 10128

My Sister's Shoppe Inc.
1671 Penfield Rd.
Rochester, NY 14625

Lasting Treasures
757 Route 25A
Rocky Point, NY 11778

Pleasure Visions
307 N. Lowell Ave.
Syracuse, NY 13204

NEVADA

Nevada Bear Co.
14 Mason Rd.
Yerington, NV 89447

OHIO

My Little Red Wagon
120 E. Mill St.
Akron, OH 44038

The Bear Necessities, Inc.
26300 Cedar Rd.
Beachwood, OH 44122

Taggart's Toys & Hobbies
11 N. Franklin St.
Chagrin Falls, OH 44022

Animal Haus Ltd.
6166 Oakhaven Dr.
Cincinnati, OH 45238

Teddy Bear Heaven
12915 Bailey Rd.
Grand Rapids, OH 43522

The Bear House
103 Jefferson St.
Greenfield, OH 45123

Carriage House
13553 State Route 31 S.
Greenfield, OH 45123

The Hearthside
6909 Hogpath Rd.
Greenville, OH 45331

Hobby Center Toys
7856 Hill Ave.
Holland, OH 43528

The Land of Make-Believe
124 N. Main St.
Hudson, OH 44236

The Attic
238 N. Main
Hudson, OH 44236

Sample's Side Door
313 Federal Ave. NE
Massillon, OH 44646

OREGON

The Old Miller Place
21358 Pacific Hwy.
Aurora, OR 97002

Puddle City Workshop
3812 SE Malden
Portland, OR 97202

Daisey Kingdom
217 NW Davis
Portland, OR 97209

HugWest
3407 SE 64th
Portland, OR 97206

Bizaar Imports
1012 Clackman's Town Ctr.
Portland, OR 97266

PENNSYLVANIA

Today & Yesterday
443 N. 11th St.
Allentown, PA 18102

Harper General Store
Route 2
Annville, PA 17003

The Bear Fax
1458 County Line Rd.
Huntington Valley,
PA 19006

Rumpelstiltskin Toy Shop
111 S. Main St.
New Hope, PA 18938

Bear Necessities
Station Square
Pittsburgh, PA 15219

Newman's
316 South St.
Philadelphia, PA 19107

The Total Teddy
640 Fern Ave.
Reading, PA 19611

RHODE ISLAND

Bear Flair
262 New Meadow Rd.
Barrington, RI 02806

The Bear Necessities, Inc.
288A Thayer St.
Providence, RI 02903

Bear Necessities
215 Goddard Row
Newport, RI 02840

SOUTH DAKOTA

The Whistle Stop
616 St. Joseph St.
Rapid City, SD 57701

TEXAS

Collectiques
2402 W. Seventh St.
Austin, TX 78703

Susan's Bear Cupboard
214 Forrest
Cleburne, TX 76031

The Hobby Horse
5310 Junius St.
Dallas, TX 75214

Teddy Bear Country
108 W. Exchange Ave.
Fort Worth, TX 76106

Scarlett O's
18910 Oak Bower Rd.
Humble, TX 77346

Stuf'd 'N Stuff
10001 Westheimer #1450
Houston, TX 77042

Critters
636 Hawthorne
Houston, TX 77006

Playhouse Toys Inc.
9433 Kirby Dr.
Houston, TX 77054

Bear Fair
2610 Salem Ave.
Lubbock, TX 79410

Noah's Ark Inc.
1100 Collin Creek Mall
Plano, TX 75075

*When your person is away,
the whole world
seems depopulated.*

The World According to HUG

The Climbing Bear
312 N. Presa St.
San Antonio, TX 78205

UTAH

**Clown Capers
and Bear Bottoms**
3749 Atmore Rd.
W. Jordan, UT 84084

VERMONT

The Hugging Bear
Main St.
Chester, VT 05143

The Rosebud Toy Co.
Candle Village
E. Arlington, VT 05252

Enchanted Doll House
4501 Deer Meadow
Manchester Ctr., VT 05255

VIRGINIA

Why Not, Inc.
200 King St.
Alexandria, VA 22314

Granny's Place
303 Cameron St.
Alexandria, VA 22314

Country Bear
14 Loudoun St. SE
Leesburg, VA 22075

Bear Hugs
8509-B Barrett Dr.
Manassas, VA 22110

The Toy Shoppe
1003 Sycamore Square Dr.
Midlothian, VA 23113

Chipmunk Hollow
Highway 211
Sperryville, VA 22740

WASHINGTON

Bear Mama's House
NE 571 Matthew Dr.
Belfair, WA 98528

**The Teddy Bear Corner
at Paul's Pharmacy**
Sheridan Village
Bremerton, WA 98310

The Honey Bear
23 Front St., Mariner Ct.
Coupeville, WA 98239

The Reminder Shop
211 Fifth Ave. N.
Edmonds, WA 98020

Bears and Bunnies
409 Main St.
Edmonds, WA 98020

Holly Haus
First Ave.
Poulsbo, WA 98370

Christopher House Toys
7010 35th Ave. NE
Seattle WA 98115

Christopher House Toys
1800 Fourth Ave.
Seattle, WA 98101

Lucy & Me
606 Yale Ave. N.
Seattle, WA 98109

Bear Hugs
7902 27th St. W.
Tacoma, WA 98466

Raggity Ann's
136 121st St. E.
Tacoma, WA 98445

WEST VIRGINIA

Little Portions Treasurers
47 Washington Ave.
Wheeling, WV 26003

WISCONSIN

The Puzzlebox
230 State St.
Madison, WI 53703

Village Bear Shop
5923 Exchange St.
McFarland, WI 53558

Finch's Nest
2120 E. Moreland Blvd.
Waukesha, WI 53703

Apriesnigs
2325 S. 64th St.
W. Allis, WI 63219

HUG says: Don't forget
to enclose a **SASE**.

Self
Addressed
Stamped
Envelope

The trick is to be proud
without having pride.

The World According to HUG

If silence is golden,
it's fool's gold.

The World According to HUG

The Mail-Order Bear: Smiles & Sorrows

Buying a Teddy Bear through a mail-order catalog can be a delightful experience and a surprising adventure. For the rural collector, the shut-in, or the just plain lazy, sending away for a mail-order Teddy Bear is a way of getting out to shop.

Poring over the colorful pictures and illustrations in the mail-order catalogs is akin to window shopping or browsing in a good bookstore. The delightful images flood your imagination with tantalizing messages. Usually, the message is 'buy me.'

Most Teddy Bear stores provide a mailing service at no extra charge except the cost of shipping. Many of these stores, like *Bear Necessities* and others, have a special mail-order catalog that you can send away for (usually at a nominal charge).

Then there are the specialty houses that sell only through the mail. Here is where the sorrows may begin. While the vast majority of Teddy Bear mail-order houses are honest, delightful to do business with and do not intend to cheat you, there are a few whose bad reputations are justly deserved.

> *Just because
> a thing is expensive
> doesn't mean it has value.*
>
> The World According to HUG

Every barrel has its rotten apple, but this shouldn't cause us to lose sight of the bright, sweet taste of the good ones. That's the way it is with mail order. There are by far more rosy apples than stinkers; and my experiences have been mostly smiles. So, I recommend shopping by mail when you can't get to the store in person.

Helpful Hints for Mail-Order Shoppers

1. Ask your friends or club members for recommendations.

2. You can not judge a book by its cover...a slick presentation is no guarantee of honesty any more than a typed sheet indicates a lack of quality.

3. Start off small. Try an inexpensive item from the catalog first. If everything works out, try another more expensive one. If it doesn't, your first loss was a small one.

4. Every state has different laws governing mail-order transactions. Find out what your state regulations are, especially regarding refunds and delivery time.

5. A good mail-order house will guarantee its products and always grant a return privilege. Do not buy from one that doesn't!

6. If you buy on a layaway plan, be sure that there are no hidden interest charges and check your return rights. Many layaway plans have a no return—no refund policy.

7. Use a personal check whenever possible. The company may insist on waiting for your check to clear before shipping the order. However, your cancelled check is still the best proof that you paid and they accepted your order. Also write a brief description of the item on the back of the check in the space where the endorsement usually goes. By endorsing the check under this little contract, the company has acknowledged your order for the goods named. Money orders do not offer you this same kind of protection. As for credit cards, using them over the phone can be risky business and one of the really great sorrows!

8. When ordering, be specific. If you will accept an alternate, say so. If not, make that very clear. If you have a special request, like a bear with close-set eyes, be just as specific here. Most companies want to be helpful and keep you as a happy, repeat customer.

9. Enclose a self-addressed stamped envelope (SASE) with your order in case a return or refund is necessary. You may get your response or refund faster if you do.

10. Be patient. Mail order takes time, usually four to six weeks. Don't start calling or writing letters after a week has gone by; it could actually delay the process. Just sit back and wait. Remember all good things come to he who waits.

Once you start ordering by mail, you will have to control yourself. The experience is always like a spontaneous Christmas. The package arrives when you least expect it and suddenly this terrific Teddy pops out of a box and makes your day. Or, it could be a pig in a poke. Like the man said, the smiles and the sorrows. ♥

Mail-Order Sources

The Grizzlies
Route 1, Box 410
Elberta, AL 36530

Carol Carlton
Box 159
Altaville, CA 95221

Echoes of the Past
2565 S. Mayflower
Arcadia, CA 91006

Critters
17200 Ventura Blvd.
Encino, CA 91316

Little Brown Bear
P.O. Box 42525
San Francisco, CA 94142

Just Bearly Enterprises
1606 Stonewood Ct.
San Pedro, CA 90732

Beary Wonderful
P.O. Box 8487
Santa Cruz, CA 95061

Teddy Bear's Picnic
122 Oak Lane
Scotts Valley, CA 95066

Fox Run
710 Holbrook
Simi Valley, CA 93065

Teddy & Friends
P.O. Box 3182
Torrance, CA 90510

The Fantasy Den
25 Morehouse Ave.
Stratford, CT 06497

My Bears
825 Bonita Dr.
Winter Park, FL 32789

Jennie's Bear Den
40 Castle Coombe
Bourbonnais, IL 60914

Bear Packets
22 Hamilton Rd.
Arlington, MA 01274

Bear Necessities
BN Mail Order Inc.
24 Union Wharf
Boston, MA 02109

Bear-In-Mind
73 Indian Pipe Lane
Concord, MA 01742

H&J Foulke
Box 310
Beltsville, MD 20705

The Bear Tender
5935 Lyndale Ave. N.
Brooklyn Center, MN 55430

Bell Enterprises
P.O. Box 366
Brooklyn, NY 11209

Marty's Miniatures
8541 Lakeshore Rd.
Clay, NY 13041

Old Time Teddy Bears
304 SE 87th Ave.
Portland, OR 97216

Original Kuddle Bear
P.O. Box 6214
Spartanburg, SC 29304

**Whistful Bears
of Whidbey Island**
924 Edgecliff Dr.
Langley, WA 98260

Vicki Burton
230 N. Mountain View
Yerington, NV 89447

Beckett's Originals
Route 1, Box 41-1A
Deerlodge, TN 37726

Merrily Supply Co.
8542 Ranchito Ave.
Panorama, CA 91402

Tiney Teddies
207 W. 55th St., Dept TT
Austin, TX 78751

Puzzle Solutions

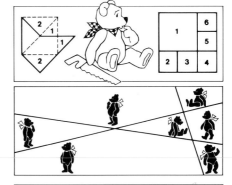

All three bears are the same size.

The great man is he who does not lose his child's heart.

...Mencius